To Maks
From Ede

INDOOR PLANTS

INDOOR PLANTS

VIOLET STEVENSON

Illustrated by
Wendy Bramall

Consultant
William Davidson

Kingfisher Books

First published in 1980.
This edition published in 1984 by Kingfisher Books Limited
Elsley Court, 20–22 Great Titchfield Street, London W1P 7AD

© Kingfisher Books Limited 1980

All Rights Reserved

BRITISH LIBRARY CATALOGUING IN PUBLICATION DATA
Stevenson, Violet
  Indoor plants. – (Kingfisher guides)
  1. House plants
  I. Title
  635.9'65   SB419
  ISBN 0 86272 085 0

Edited by Julia Kirk
Colour separations by Newsele Litho, Milan, London
Printed and bound in Italy by Vallardi Industrie
Grafiche, Milan

CONTENTS

Introduction	9
Foliage Plants	26
Ferns	76
Palms	82
Flowering Plants	85
Cacti and Succulents	106
Bulbous Plants	118
Glossary	122
Index	123

INTRODUCTION

Origins of house plants

It is only possible to guess who were the first growers of house plants. We know that the Egyptians grew plants in their homes thousands of years ago. The records they left show scented plants growing in pots in the courtyards and inner chambers of wealthy traders and royal families. We know that the Romans were also skilled pot gardeners; murals show indoor plants being watched and watered with obvious interest.

Plant explorers

In the nineteenth century there was a burst of discovery on the plant scene. Plant "explorers" began collecting new and unknown species from all over the world, an activity which produced an important discovery.

So many plants were lost in the hazardous and lengthy journeys across the world that it became necessary to find some means of packing that would protect the plants and allow them to grow during their long trip. Dr. Nathaniel Ward came up with the answer – a completely sealed case made almost entirely of glass. This prevented sea spray, cold winds and polluted air from injuring or contaminating the plants, yet allowed them the light they needed.

A brightly-coloured indoor display of leaves and flowers.

Steam heat

A second important factor in the development of the house plant industry was the introduction of hot water systems for heating. It became possible to heat a greenhouse or a 'stove' house in such a way that it could reproduce the hot, humid conditions of the tropics. From the stove houses came other heated greenhouses and also the conservatory, a heated and humidified glass-roofed room which was a part of the house.

The strange and exotic plants being brought back from the tropics could now be safely grown by those who could afford heated conservatories. Later it was discovered that there were, in fact, certain plants which would grow in their smoke-filled, gas-lit rooms. Plants such as the Aspidistra from Japan, the Rubber Plant from India and some palms from the East Indies became popular symbols of those stuffy and respectable days.

New times, new plants

As times changed even the wealthy could no longer afford stove houses or conservatories. Electricity became the common and clean method of lighting and central heating made it possible to provide constant temperatures all year round.

NAMING PLANTS

Definitions

A true house plant can be defined as one which is grown under normal home conditions for a period of more than four seasons. However, this definition eliminates practically every flowering plant, all bulbs and seasonal plants such as Poinsettia and Geranium, so the definition has been expanded a little to take in what can be called "temporary" plants. These are plants which can be grown indoors for a limited period, for example, during the flowering season, and then replaced in the greenhouse or garden. It is possible, for example, to dig up a clump of crocuses from the garden, keep them indoors for a few days and then return them to their original home.

Although flowering plants have a brief life in flower, they can still be enjoyed during this time. Many other plants which produce their flowers as a mere seasonal burst provide interesting, decorative foliage all year round.

Types of house plants

House plants can broadly be divided into four major types: foliage plants, flowering plants, cacti and succulents and bulbous plants. But of course these can be sub-divided into more specific categories.

For instance, foliage plants include climbing and bushy varieties as well as trailers and tree-like plants. Flowering plants can be divided into temporary, semi-permanent and true house plants, the last category depending on the foliage.

There are many species within each group available to the indoor gardener. The cacti and succulents group contains many species that fit neatly into the classification of house plants, but in the bulbous flowering plants group only a handful out of hundreds can be chosen, largely on the basis of popularity.

Because of the huge range of indoor plants, any book on the subject is necessarily limited in scope and it is possible to deal here with only a representative selection of those plants available.

Common names or Latin?

Ask the average person to describe a daisy and he or she will tell you that it has a number of white

Foliage plants　　**Flowering plants**

petals surrounding a golden centre and that it can be small or large. This description covers several hundred plants, all of which are or can be called daisies. But the name *Bellis perennis* refers to only one species the world over – to the common daisy.

The use of Latin names is really a question of accuracy. Common names are not precise enough and sometimes refer to more than one plant. There are Cape ivies, German ivies and Grape ivies, yet none of these is remotely connected to the true ivy, *Hedera helix*. The popular Impatiens is known as Busy Lizzie in Great Britain and Patient Lucy in the United States, and although both common names are equally correct, it is the Latin name, *Impatiens holstii*, which is recognized in all parts of the world for one plant only. It may be easier and more amusing to remember a plant by the name of Mother-in-Law's Tongue than by the complicated botanical name of *Sansevieria trifasciata laurentii* as long as it is realized that accuracy is sometimes essential.

Latin is easy

Some correct botanical names may not come easily to the tongue, but they are so logical that once the basic process of their use is accepted it is difficult to go wrong.

By agreement between botanists all over the world all botanical names are printed and used in exactly the same way in Latin, and are always printed in italics. The first name, which begins with a capital letter, is the genus, or group, which can include a large number of species, all basically similar. The various plants within a genus are called species and the species name is added to the genus name.

To take an example, *Sansevieria trifasciata laurentii*; the genus is *Sansevieria*, the species is *trifasciata*, and the sub-species or variety is *laurentii*. Where this variety or sub-species is cultivated as opposed to being a natural growth, it is known as a cultivar.

The International Committee on Horticultural Nomenclature meets regularly in various parts of the world to review plant names and discuss the naming of new strains. There are corrections continually being made, but these are of importance only to botanists.

Cacti and succulents

Bulbous plants

PLANTS IN THE HOME

Buying a house plant

Examine every new plant with great care. Most plants on sale in reputable outlets are strong and healthy and have been well looked after but an occasional rogue gets through. Look first for the obvious: for strong and sturdy growth, clean undamaged leaves and a clean and undamaged pot. Check that no leaves are yellow or brown and that leaves are not curled or twisted from insect attack. Examine carefully for signs of greenfly, whitefly or mealy bug and scale insects. Check that the soil is moist but not sodden since over-watering may cause irreparable damage.

If it is a flowering plant make sure that one or two of the flowers are open and healthy and that there are plenty of buds waiting to follow on. If you buy in winter make sure the plant is well wrapped, all parts of it, before you take it out into the cold. Remember that it has been used to a warm, humid environment.

When you get your new plant home the first thing to do is water it thoroughly. Place it in a bucket of water and wait until all the bubbles have ceased rising from the soil surface before taking it out again and allowing it to drain.

How a plant works

The requirements for a plant to grow strong and healthy are very similar to those of our own: food, water, warmth, cleanliness and shelter, but there is one extra vital need – it must have light. This is the most important element in its life. Light is necessary for the manufacture of sugars which the plant consumes for its immediate energy requirements and stores in the form of starches.

Water is also a vital need. Water drawn up through the roots serves two main purposes. First it dissolves plant foods into solutions which can be absorbed by the plant and these are sent up through stems and leaves. Water also keeps the plant cells turgid to allow moisture to evaporate from the leaves so they can transpire and keep cool.

Transpiration

In hot weather, in full sun or in arid conditions some plants will transpire so quickly that the roots are unable to absorb enough moisture quickly enough to send it through the plant veins. When this happens the turgid cells soften and collapse, making it even more difficult for water to travel through them. The answer is to reduce the transpiration rate by removing the plant from the source of heat, by increasing humidity or by adding moisture artificially to the outer leaves. Unless the soil is obviously dry it is of no value to add water in the hope that this will travel up through the plant, for only so much can be absorbed at a time.

Plant leaves can become very dusty in the home and a layer of dirt will clog the pores and prevent efficient transpiration. Large and shiny leaves can be cleaned with tepid water and a soft sponge. Smaller or soft leaves (with exceptions) need spraying and best of all for them is a period in a soft summer rain shower to clean off household dirt.

Over-watering

If plants are placed outdoors make sure that the rain can drain through the pot. Over-watering will kill almost every plant because roots need to breathe and if all the air spaces in the soil are filled with water the plant will drown. More plants die from over-watering than from any other treatment. It is a simple matter to give a little more water or food, but a difficult and lengthy process to remove excess water or food from the soil.

How a plant works

Photosynthesis

Carbon dioxide

Sunlight

Chlorophyll

Oxygen

During the process of photosynthesis, carbon dioxide, absorbed through the stomata from the air, combines with water and chlorophyll to to make carbohydrates which are stored in the roots. Oxygen is given off as a by-product of this process.

Water

Stomata

Transpiration

Sugar and starches to roots

Water is drawn up through the stem and transpires through the stomata on the epidermis of leaves to keep the plant cool. This process is known as transpiration.

PLANT NEEDS

Light
The most important ingredient of good health in a house plant is light. Even in a modern house with large windows the loss of light compared with outdoors is surprising.

Quantity of light differs in summer and winter. Only the toughest of cacti and succulents can stand hours of hot summer sun, but many plants can well do with winter sunshine, weaker in strength and shorter in duration.

Flowering plants and foliage plants with variegated leaves must have good light to maintain their colour. All green plants need less light and as a rule the darker the green and the thicker the leaves the less light they will need.

Artificial light can be used to supplement daylight for some plants in winter and certain plants such as African violets can be grown entirely in artificial light.

Warmth
Almost all house plants need protection from frost and from temperatures of more than about 24°C (75°F). Most will grow in or adapt to a well-lit, moderately humid room which is maintained at about 18-21°C (64-70°F), a comfortable living warmth. However, many winter plants such as Azalea, Cyclamen and Poinsettia grow better and last longer in cool rooms rather than those that are too warm.

Water
It must be repeated that more plants are killed by over-watering than by any other means. Only

Light needs of some plants

Full sun	Very light	Light	Some shade	Deep shade
Cacti	Abutilon	Achimenes	Acorus	All ferns
Pelargonium	African violet	Anthurium	Aralia	Fittonia
Sansevieria	Araucaria	Aphelandra	Aspidistra	Ficus pumila
	Bougainvillea	Begonia	Cissus	Hedera helix
Some Sun	Calceolaria	Caladium	Fatshedera	varieties
	Campanula	Columnea	Ficus elastica	Helxine
Aechmea	Chlorophytum	Cyclamen	Hedera	Philodendron
Ananas	Chrysanthemum	Dracaena	canariensis	scandens
Begonia rex	Cineraria	Erica	Maranta	
Billbergia	Codiaeum	Hoya	Philodendrons	
Citrus	Fuchsia	Hypocyrta	Platycerium	
Coleus	Gloxinia	Iresine	Rhoicissus	
Cordyline	Hydrangea	Plectranthus	Scindapsus	
Cryptanthus	Monstera	Primula	Stromanthe	
Impatiens	Saxifraga		Tradescantia	
Jasmine	Solanum		Zebrina	
Palms				
Vriesia				

A cache pot provides a layer of water-absorbent material, such as peat, around the plant.

Humidity can also be provided by standing plants on a bed of gravel, half-covered with water.

A spray with tepid water will help to maintain humidity in a hot, dry atmosphere.

water or marsh plants such as Cyperus should be allowed to rest in water and only cacti and some succulents should be allowed to go entirely bone dry for periods.

The best way to tell if a plant needs water is to gently test the soil surface. If you can feel any moisture do not water. Allow most plants almost to dry out before applying water again and then make sure that the whole of the root ball has been moistened, not just the upper surface. Never allow a no-soil or peat-based rooting medium to become totally dry or it will be very difficult to moisten thoroughly again.

Humidity

In a humid atmosphere plants will not transpire as quickly as they will in dry air and they will need less water at the roots. Too dry air is bad for the plants and encourages red spider mites, a pest difficult to clear and capable of doing much damage.

In summer a degree of humidity can be obtained merely by opening a window, but in winter the air in a modern home can become very dry and damaging. A humidifier can make a considerable difference to the plants yet have no effect on humans, and spraying plants with tepid water will also help. Practically all plants should stand in a cache pot filled with moist peat or on a tray with moist gravel, for both of these will send up a mini-cloud of moisture around the leaves.

GENERAL CARE

Feeding and fertilizers

All newly acquired house plants should have enough food in their soil to last them for a short period after purchase, but continue to feed regularly during the growing season. Plants should receive only a quarter of their summer feeding dose in winter when they are resting. Always under- rather than over-feed. Over-feeding can burn or otherwise damage plant roots.

House plant fertilizers can take several forms. First of all, there are the basic chemicals in powder or crystal form, to be made up into a solution at the correct rate and applied to the soil surface. Probably more convenient is the liquid fertilizer, to be diluted and applied to the plant soil, or the solid which is sprinkled onto the soil surface and watered in.

There is also a very simple method in the form of a tablet, which is pushed into the soil and will slowly disintegrate. Foliar feeds, that are sprayed onto the plant foliage, are also effective.

Pruning

At one time or another, certain plants will outgrow their situation and will have to be cut back. Careful pruning will then be needed to control their size. It is also helpful with many house plants to 'stop' them or pinch out the growing tips. This encourages attractive, bushy growth instead of a straggly appearance, but bear in mind that when a growing tip has been pinched out the plant has received a shock, so reduce water and food until new growth indicates that the plant has recovered. Pinching out a tender growing tip can usually be done with the finger nails. A sharp knife, efficient secateurs or good kitchen scissors

'Pinching out' can usually be done with the fingertips. The result is stronger, bushier growth and the production of more flowers.

Training plants — Trellis, Hoop, Hanging basket, Mossed pole

should be used for firmer or more woody growth to get a clean cut that will not invite the attention of any fungus spores.

Training

Some plants can be controlled in their growth by training rather than stopping. A climber can be encouraged to grow up a trellis or a rope, perhaps by tying it in position as it grows upwards. Some climbers with aerial roots can be trained to climb a cane or a moss pole.

Epiphytic plants, which grow on trees in their original jungle habitat, can often be nailed or tied to a tree trunk or a piece of cork bark and will grow there quite happily. They must be in a position where they can easily be watered, or they should be taken down and watered at intervals.

Grooming

At some time most house plants will produce the odd dead flower, brown leaf or awkward aerial root. Better and more attractive plants result if they are given regular grooming to remove debris and cut away the eyesores.

When plants are groomed to remove dead leaves or any other eyesores, the leaves that remain should be cleaned of the dust that almost certainly has fallen upon them. Large leaves can be cleaned individually with a soft sponge and clean, tepid water.

Smaller leaves and foliage of such plants as cacti and ferns can present problems. Spray if possible or take outside to enjoy a summer shower. The hairy-leaved plants should not be washed. Instead, use a soft brush to get rid of dust.

PESTS AND DISEASES

Prevention
Most bad pest infestations and most plant "illnesses" can be prevented. A strong, healthy plant will resist trouble where a weakly plant might go down under attack. So make sure your plants never become diseased. Regulate watering and feeding carefully and use only sterilized soil preparations. Keep soil surfaces clear of fallen and decayed foliage.

It is also a good idea to examine all plants carefully at regular intervals and remove to quarantine any plant that looks sickly, since diseases can quickly spread to healthy plants. Keep air circulating to prevent fungus spores settling.

Pests
House plant pests are normally very few in number and one can grow plants for many years without much trouble. Perhaps the most common pest to be seen is the familiar greenfly, which can be seen with the naked eye on the tender growing tips of the plant. As well as causing twisting and mottling of the leaves, the greenfly also produce a honeydew secretion. There are many good sprays available which will quickly clear the pest.

Less easy to identify and almost impossible to see are the red spider mites which attack certain plants, notably ivies, in hot, dry conditions. The mites reveal themselves by the presence of soft white webs on the undersides of some leaves. Otherwise leaves turn yellow and curl or become brittle and papery. Spray thoroughly, particularly the undersides of the leaves, with liquid derris or some other suitable proprietary insecticide. Try to increase humidity as a preventive measure.

Mealy bug is easier to see, for it consists of a tiny brown insect that wraps itself in a comparatively large wad of cotton wool. The difficulty is that the pests find the most awkward joints and cracks to hide in. Once discovered they can be dealt with easily enough by dipping a soft paint brush in methylated spirits and touching the wool with this. The white, fluffy exterior disappears and the little brown insect is killed.

Leaf spot, a fungal disease, clearly shown on the leaves of **Hedera helix.**

The appearance of many tiny white specks, usually on the undersides of leaves, may indicate an infestation of white fly, a difficult pest to clear. Like greenfly, they also produce a sticky and clearly visible honeydew. If only one or two small plants are attacked it is possible to kill the flies by sealing the plant and pot inside a polythene bag for a day or two, although this may not clear the eggs which may have been laid. But usually one must resort to the unpleasant and difficult process of spraying, using malathion or liquid derris. Make sure both sides of all affected leaves are drenched with the solution.

Watch also for scale insects, light brown and flat, which attach themselves to leaves and suck the sap. They cling tightly but can be removed by a knife blade or by wiping with cotton wool soaked in methylated spirit.

Pesticides

For those who dislike or disapprove of chemical pesticides, many pests can be cleared with plain water or soapy water. Spray or merely dip the affected part. If chemical sprays are used, remember always that these are poisons. Use them only out of doors or close off a room after use. Wear rubber gloves and wash carefully after use.

Diseases

Diseases of house plants are rare

The drastic effects of root and stem rot on Cineraria. Both plants are the same age, one wilting due to infection, the other healthy.

and with reasonable care should never be seen. The most common are botrytis, a grey mould, certain mildews, certain rusts and a few virus diseases. Botrytis can appear on any part of a plant, usually where the air is cool, still and moist. Spray with a fungicide and increase ventilation. Mildews also show as moulds, usually whiter, and can be cleared by fungicides and prevented with better ventilation. Rusts and fungi are easily seen and identified, and can be cleared by dithane.

Virus diseases may be brought in by a sick plant or on hands or clothing. They are too difficult to be handled by the average amateur and when virus attack has been diagnosed the best thing to do is remove and burn the affected plants at once.

SOILS AND POTTING

Types of pot

In the past 20 years or so there has been a swing away from the traditional clay flower pot to plastic pots. Reasons for this are that plastic is cheaper, lighter in weight, less breakable and more easily cleaned. These are strong arguments in favour, but against are the facts that clay breathes, it absorbs and releases moisture, it has a relationship with soil and it is heavy enough to be considerably more stable than plastic. Pots of both materials are similar in shape and size, although the plastic pot usually carries a number of small drainage holes in the base instead of the single larger one of clay.

Soils

As mentioned earlier it is not recommended that garden soil or even rich home-made compost should be used for house plants unless these can be sterilized to kill all weeds and harmful organisms. It is much more convenient and worthwhile to use specially prepared composts, normally available at all good garden stores. These are a specially prepared blend of loam, peat and sand, and there are several kinds, ranging from seed compost and potting compost and increasing in strength of built-in fertilizer. There are also a number of 'no-soil' composts made from a sterile peat base and with added fertilizer.

In addition to these two basic types of 'manufactured' soils there are such products as vermiculite and perlite, both lightweight minerals capable of absorbing many times their own weight of moisture, yet being well drained.

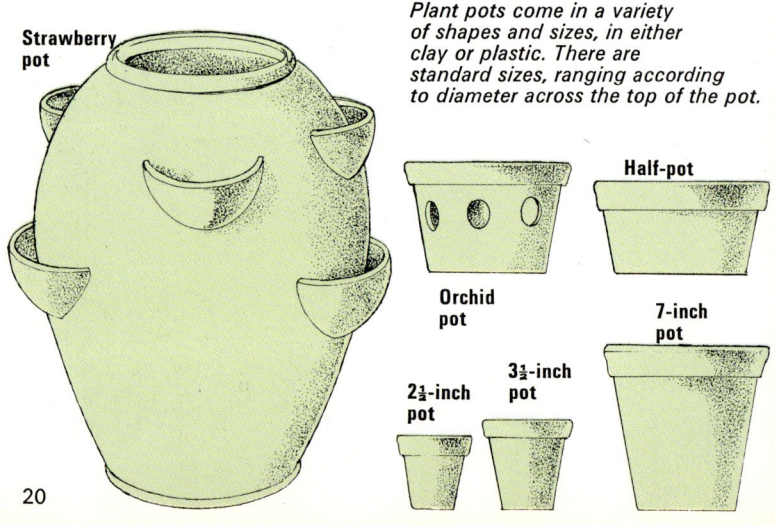

Plant pots come in a variety of shapes and sizes, in either clay or plastic. There are standard sizes, ranging according to diameter across the top of the pot.

Strawberry pot

Half-pot

Orchid pot

7-inch pot

2½-inch pot

3½-inch pot

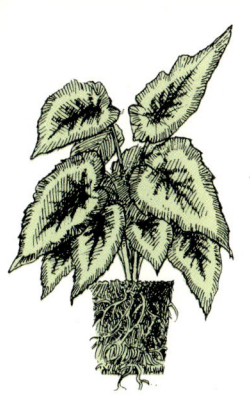  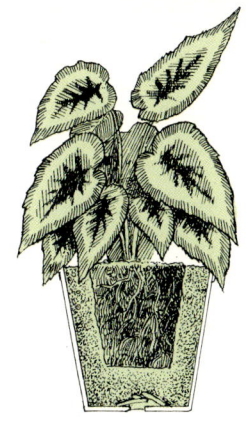

If roots fill the pot, knock out the plant keeping the root ball intact.

Place the pot inside a slightly larger one and fill around with good growing soil.

Remove the inner pot, placing the root ball in position, firm around and water.

Hydroponics

Although over-watering drowns plant roots, paradoxically it is possible to grow plants in water alone without soil. The answer is that some of the roots must be able to breathe air.

One simple yet highly efficient system that has been working for several years without a single failure is to suspend the plant roots in a wire mesh tray at the top of a green glass container so that they fall through into the water below and hold the plant firmly in position. In one or two weeks, according to season and weather, the water level will have dropped so that a large proportion of the roots will be dry and capable of breathing air, though in an enclosed and humid atmosphere. The water level is then topped up so that the roots are submerged again.

More sophisticated and foolproof systems exist, which make use of purpose-made pots and a special growing medium of large clay granules.

Puddle pots

By taking hydroponics one stage further into the decorative and propagative fields, one reaches a product known as the 'puddle pot'. In effect this is a decorative container without drainage holes which is filled with small pebbles and water. Tip cuttings are taken from plants such as ivies, Cissus, Rhoicissus, Chlorophytum and many others and these are inserted between the pebbles in the puddle pot. They soon form roots and grow so that the pot becomes, in effect, a mixed arrangement of young plants. They can be potted up or added to at any time.

TAKING CUTTINGS

A softwood or stem cutting of Pelargonium has the lower leaves removed. It is inserted about half way in the soil with any remaining leaves above the surface.

Methods of propagation

Of the many ways of propagating plants the sowing of seed is probably the best known, but is the least suited to the house plant grower, who wishes to have not 50 plants but one. However, there are other ways of propagating plants.

Perhaps the easiest way is to use the plant's own system. For example, many bromeliads send up offshoots which can be cut away with a portion of root and potted up. Chlorophytum plants grow tiny plantlets on the ends of long stems and these will grow if pegged down into soil. There are plants which grow in clumps, such as African Violets, and these can be teased gently apart to make several new plants. Many bulbs multiply by growing smaller bulbs, which can be picked off and grown on for a year or two until ready to flower.

Cuttings

Softwood or tip cuttings should be up to 52 mm (2 in) long with several nodes. Strip off leaves and insert base in growing medium. Hardwood cuttings are usually longer but much the same.

Leaf cuttings are of several kinds. African Violet leaves can be removed and the stalk placed in the soil or in plain water. Begonia leaves can be cut into several pieces and each planted. Sansevierias can be cut into 5 cm (2 in) lengths and inserted in

The convenient Chlorophytum produces its own baby plants on the ends of long stems. These are pegged down into the soil and stems are cut when the baby plants start growing.

the soil, but this will not produce plants with the golden line, these must be divided from roots. Begonia leaves can also be laid flat on the soil with cut major veins and plants will grow at these points.

Certain climbers such as ivies and Cissus can have a trail led away to another pot. If at this point the stem is half broken or sliced partly through, this portion can be buried in the soil and a new plant will grow. This is known as layering.

Air layering is useful for upright plants which cannot be led along to another pot. A Rubber Plant, for example, can have a similar nick or slice made in the main stem some 15 cm (6 in) or so below the tip. Wet sphagnum moss can be packed around this and tied in place and covered with polythene sheeting or a plastic bag, also tied in place. Roots will grow into this and when new growth is seen at the top the portion below the package can be cut away.

Sansevieria *leaves can be cut into portions and planted in soil. Clip Sansevieria sections at the end which was originally nearest the base of the leaf and put this end in the soil.*

Aids to propagation

Use sterilized soil or growing medium and make sure that pots, knives, scissors or any other tools used are spotlessly clean, even preferably sterile. A great aid to propagation is hormone rooting powder or liquid which hastens the rooting of cuttings. Merely dip the tip to be rooted in the powder or liquid, then pot up the cutting.

A small propagating case with facilities for gentle bottom heat and enclosure to get good humidity will make the raising of cuttings almost foolproof. Otherwise, good results can be obtained by placing the potted cuttings inside a polythene bag.

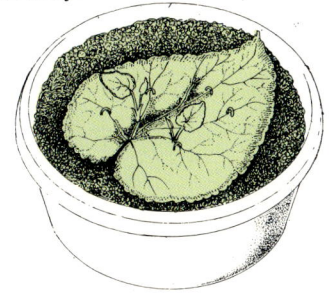

Begonia rex *can be propagated by pegging down the leaf on soil with cuts made in main veins.*

BOTTLE GARDENS

Pretty and practical

Apart from the visual appeal of bottle gardens and terrariums, there are also advantages for the plants growing inside. As well as being protected from gas fumes, dry air and draughts, the plants also enjoy a little micro-climate of humidity of their own.

These special gardens are not difficult to make, although they may demand a considerable attention to detail and a delicacy of handling. It is important to start off with young, small plants which will not outgrow their restricted environment. The soil or growing medium must be rich enough to sustain the plants but not so rich that it encourages strong growth. Above all, watering must be carried out carefully, preferably with a spray. The soil should be moist, but not wet. The balance between water, soil and plants is a delicate one and may take several attempts before a successful micro-climate is established.

Cases and containers

A terrarium can be improvized from any unwanted container such as a discarded fish tank, an old glass battery case or some similar container which is waterproof and will admit as much light as possible. It must be large enough to accept more than just one or two plants but not so large that it will become something of a jungle. Decorative features can also be included, such as a rock or two and perhaps a piece of driftwood.

Drainage material, such as charcoal, should go in before being covered by a layer of potting compost.

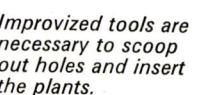

Improvized tools are necessary to scoop out holes and insert the plants.

Once firmed down, the plants can be sprayed lightly to ensure adequate moisture and humidity.

Drainage must be good. A base of an inch or two of gravel will be sufficient, on top of which soil should be added to a suitable depth.

Planning a bottle garden

These are usually made from large, industrial glass containers with a small neck. Because of the narrow neck, several problems must be overcome and a completed bottle garden shows ingenuity and inventiveness as well as decorative flair. A problem here that does not appear with a more open terrarium is the cleanliness of the interior. It must be spotlessly clean to look attractive but it is not easy to devise cleaning tools that will reach every part of the interior.

Once clean, the bottle can be filled. The drainage material should go in first, preferably through a funnel of some kind, which can be improvised from a piece of card or paper. The soil can then be poured in next, and this will look better if made into one or two hills and valleys rather than a flat plain.

Certain specialized tools will be needed for planting and these are best devised by the user according to his special skills. One implement is necessary for scooping holes, another for covering roots and firming soil, and also important is a tool to move plants and pick up any pieces of debris such as a fallen leaf.

An arrangement of driftwood may help to create a well-balanced 'landscape'. When the planting has been completed trickle minimal quantities of water down the sides to wash down dust. Place out of sun but in good light. Do not seal.

Plants suitable for bottle gardens:

Begonia rex
Carex japonica
Codiaeum
Cryptanthus
Hedera helix
Fittonia argyroneura
Maranta
Pellionia pulchra
Peperomia caperata
Peperomia magnoliaefolia
  variegata
Pilea cadierei
Pteris cretica
Saintpaulia

FOLIAGE PLANTS

What makes indoor gardening different from all other aspects of horticulture is the emphasis on foliage plants. All real house plants are evergreen, meaning that they hold their leaves through summer and winter. 'Evergreen', in fact, can mean almost any colour except a true blue, and two or more colours are often mixed in a single leaf. Within the range of foliage plants there are many colourful and decorative varieties which will retain their interest the whole year round.

Acorus

ACORUS

(*Acorus gramineus*)
Family Araceae. A genus of two species of perennial water herbs from many parts of the world.
Habit: erect, compact tufts of upright growing grass, 20-25 cm (8-10 in) tall.
Description: a marsh grass, needing to be constantly wet. The type is all green but there is a variegated form, *A. g. variegatus.* Best grown standing in water.
Needs: soil permanently saturated with water. Good light but not direct sun for long periods.
Dangers: the soil of Acorus should never be allowed to dry out or the roots will shrivel and the plant will die.
Uses: as a contrast in leaf shape or in an indoor water garden.
Propagation: roots can be prised apart and potted up at any time of the year. Stand young plants in puddles of water.

CHINESE EVERGREEN

(*Aglaonema commutatum*)
Family Araceae. A genus of about 25 species of tropical evergreen perennials with bright leaves.
Habit: Aglaonemas have large spear-shaped leaves usually striped, blotched or dotted with varied colours, growing on short stems from a central point, green, white, cream, grey.
Description: these are not easy plants to find nowadays, the best-known probably being Silver Queen with leaves in tones of silver or grey. Plants will sometimes grow quite large, up to 1 m (3 ft) or so tall.
Needs: Aglaonemas will grow well enough if they are kept warm and in fairly humid conditions in the home. Although their roots should be moist, the plants must never be wet and a sharply-drained compost is essential for them. Give light shade and never direct sunlight.
Dangers: one common trouble is mealy bug, which collect at the base of the stems and are almost impossible to see. It is worth while to dribble a little pesticide down the stems every now and again to make sure that all the pests have been cleared.
Uses: a strikingly decorative plant.
Propagation: by division of the root clump, using a warm propagator.

VARIEGATED PINEAPPLE

(*Ananas bracteatus striatus*)
Family Bromeliaceae. A genus of

three species of herbaceous perennials.
Habit: a typical bromeliad, with slender leaves arching out from a central stem.
Description: the common pineapple, *A. comosus,* is a plain grey-green with wide, spined leaves. This variegated form is larger with longer,

Vivid colours and the interest of being able to see a fruit grow are advantages offered by the variegated pineapple plant.

slimmer leaves, green and gold with a pinkish tinge in the centre. After about four years a well-grown plant will send up a stem up to 60 cm (2 ft) in length bearing a vivid pink fruit and intensely blue flowers.
Needs: good light and a little warmth. Keep the roots a little on the dry side.
Dangers: the greatest danger is in allowing the roots to stay wet too long.
Uses: a highly decorative plant for the home. Beware of needle sharp leaf endings which can be dangerous.
Propagation: side shoots will appear when a plant has fruited and these can be removed when of a suitable size and treated like a cutting. A propagating case or heated greenhouse will be necessary to provide warmth and humidity.

Aglaonema commutatum

modestum

crispum

NORFOLK ISLAND PINE

(*Araucaria excelsa*)
Family Pinaceae. A genus of about ten species of tender evergreen conifers.
Habit: a tree with regular, symmetrical branches in steps, covered with many tiny bright-green leaves like pine needles.
Description: the Norfolk Island Pine is a tree from an island near New Zealand, where it will grow to 30 m (100 ft) or so. Indoors it grows slowly and will take ten years to reach 2 m (6 ft). Young growth is soft and almost downy, the tiny incurving leaves being bright-green at first and later turning to a grey-green. It is the regularity of growth, the evenly-spaced and well-proportioned branches that give a special elegance to this plant.
Needs: this is an easy plant to grow in the home as long as it is not subjected to extreme warmth and dryness of air. It is not hardy, but will grow happily in temperatures lower than humans enjoy. It likes a little humidity, so a gentle spray with tepid water is beneficial.
Dangers: hot, dry air; cold, wet roots. The growing medium must be open and free-draining and can be almost dry in winter.
Uses: this shapely, graceful, elegant conifer is ideal for home decoration, where it should be allowed to stand alone to be admired. It will not drop its leaves unless the atmosphere is dry.
Propagation: Araucaria is said to grow well from seed, but the only seed generally available is of another species, *A. araucana*, the Monkey Puzzle Tree. Tip cuttings can be rooted in some warmth.

CAST IRON PLANT

(*Aspidistra elatior*)
Family Liliaceae. A genus of about four species of evergreen, perennial herbs.
Habit: long, dark-green, spear-shaped leaves rise from a sturdy, short stalk.

In its native home near New Zealand the Norfolk Island Pine, Araucaria excelsa, will grow up to 30 m (100 ft) tall, but when confined to a pot and given artificial living conditions it will seldom grow to more than 2 m or so in several years, when it is at its best.

Description: the Aspidistra was at one time so common a plant that it aroused derision and amusement and eventually went out of fashion. It is a slow grower and supplies are not easily available. The variegated form with white vertical stripes, is even more difficult to find. Aspidistra gained popularity simply because it was one of the few plants that could grow in the gas-lit smoky, heavily-curtained Victorian home. It produces small, dark-purple flowers at soil level.
Needs: although the Aspidistra will accept poor treatment this does not mean that it must be neglected. Some warmth, a lightly-shaded situation, an ample water supply in summer and less in winter are repaid by more leaves, quicker growth and a richer

appearance. The leaves tend to become dusty in time and should be cleaned with plain water and a soft sponge. Never use any leaf shining preparation on the leaves as this will cause damage to their apparently tough and almost fibrous surface texture. Aspidistras prefer to be pot-bound rather than live in a home which is too large for them. If plants grow too big they can be divided every five years or so and if the roots are too numerous they can have the base of the root ball cut away with a sharp knife.

Dangers: frost; neglect; over-watering.

Uses: in the home it is best to make use of the plant to decorate some place where other plants fail to grow, perhaps in some darkish corner.

Propagation: by division of the suckers or offshoots. With a sharp knife merely cut the offshoots away with some roots.

Aspidistra

IRON CROSS BEGONIA

(*Begonia masoniana*)
Family Begoniaceae. A genus of about 350 succulent herbs or sub-shrubs.

Habit: typical Begonia 'lop-sided', heart-shaped leaves, crinkled and hairy, green-gold with very dark-green, almost a chocolate 'iron cross' pattern in the centre.

Begonia masoniana

Description: this distinctive Begonia is a rhizomatous type, easy to grow in the normal home. The hairy stems and crinkled leaves make it something of a dust collector, so a spell in a gentle summer rain shower is helpful. As the plant grows it puts out more and more leaves which get progressively smaller, so it is wise to take cuttings.

Needs: this Begonia must have good light but never direct sun. Normal living temperatures are suitable and there is no special need for extra humidity. The roots should be kept moist at all times but should never be really wet for long.

Dangers: cold; hot sun; cold or hot draughts; too wet a soil mixture.

Uses: this is a pleasant, decorative plant, better standing alone than with others in an arrangement or group.

Propagation: not an easy plant, but it is worth trying to raise cuttings as is done with *Begonia rex* (page 30).

BEGONIA REX

(*Begonia rex*)
Family and genus as for *B. masoniana*.
Habit: an extensive range of ornamental leaved Begonias growing from a creeping rhizome, with the characteristic 'lop-sided' heart shape and in many different combinations of colours and textures.
Description: *Begonia rex* leaves are almost all 20-30 cm (8-12 in) long and not quite so wide. They grow on a

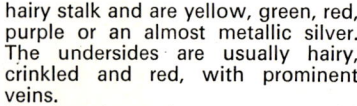

Begonia rex

The Caladium has a comparatively short season in the home, but in that time can develop into one of the most beautiful of all foliage house plants.

hairy stalk and are yellow, green, red, purple or an almost metallic silver. The undersides are usually hairy, crinkled and red, with prominent veins.
Needs: these plants are easy and tolerant to grow in the home, needing no special treatment. They sometimes become a little 'leggy' after a few years and are best discarded after new plants have been raised from them by cuttings.
Dangers: frost; too wet or too dry roots. A hot sun on the foliage will brown and burn it, particularly if wet.
Uses: *Begonia rex* plants make wonderful home decoration, for they can be used alone or in groups in most situations. If grown in rather larger pots than necessary leaves can be extra large, and on the other hand they can be kept in small pots which will restrict growth.
Propagation: by leaf cuttings in a propagating case.

ANGEL'S WINGS

(*Caladium bicolor*)
Family Araceae. A genus of about 16 species of interesting perennial herbs.
Description: this is not strictly a house plant as the foliage dies down at the end of summer, but the large leaves are so beautiful and delicate that it is well worth growing. These are held on a slender stalk and can grow to 30 cm (12 in) or more long. Colours range from a fragile and almost lacy white with green ribs to a delicate pink, green, red or any mixture of these colours — spotted, streaked or margined.

Caladium bicolor candidum

PEACOCK PLANT

(*Calathea* species)
Family Marantaceae. A genus of some 100 species of decorative perennial herbs.
Habit: leaves sometimes almost round, sometimes long and slender, magnificently coloured and on strong, thin stalks.
Description: *C. mackoyana* has silver or white and green leaves, the white almost translucent, the green in streaks and blotches, the underside purple. *C. ornata* has pink stripes in its dark green leaves and this colour changes to white as the plant matures.
Needs: all the Calatheas are difficult plants to grow well for long. They must be warm, about 18°C (65°F), fairly humid and the roots should be moist at all times though not wet. Plants protected in a bowl or bottle garden frequently grow best.
Dangers: cold and dry roots are killers as are arid conditions and draughts whether of too hot or too cold air.
Uses: Calathea is especially striking in a terrarium.
Propagation: by division of the roots, which can be merely teased apart and potted up, kept very warm and humid.

Needs: this is a delicate plant and it needs careful handling. It is a marsh plant in its tropical habitat, so the peaty soil in which it is grown in the home must always be kept moist, not quite wet but wetter than most plants would enjoy. It must also be warm — never cooler than about 16°C (61°F). Even brief periods of cold can do much damage, as can draughts of hot or cold air. At the end of summer when the foliage dies down water can gradually be withheld until the soil is dry. The tuber should then be stored, dry and warm, until it is started into growth again in early spring.
Dangers: cold and dryness at the roots must be avoided. A hot sun directly on the foliage will burn it and draughts will cause it to wilt.
Uses: a strikingly beautiful plant, to be given a place of honour in the home.
Propagation: by placing the dormant tuber in moist peat in a warm propagating case in early spring.

Calathea mackoyana

C. ornata

Callisia

CALLISIA

(*Callisia elegans*)
Family Commelinaceae. A genus of about four species of low herbs.
Habit: a trailing creeper with compact white-striped green leaves, the underside of which is an even and rich purple.
Description: this is a plant allied and similar to the familiar Tradescantia. There is another species, *C. purpurea,* which is purple throughout instead of merely on the underside of the leaves. Both are easy plants to grow indoors and both will produce long trails which can be pinched out to give a thicker, bushier plant. The pieces that are removed will root easily and it is an advantage always to keep new, young plants coming along rather than keep old plants which become thin and weary. *C. elegans* is also known as *Setcreasea striata* and *C. purpurea* as *S. purpurea.*
Needs: like Tradescantia, the Callisia is easy enough to grow in the home, requiring good light in order to retain the colour of the foliage but disliking direct sun except for very brief periods. It needs plenty of water when growing vigorously and will improve its performance if fed regularly but lightly. In winter, when growth has slowed, feeding should be stopped and watering reduced until the soil is maintained in an almost dry state.
Dangers: although this plant must be kept warm it must not be baked nor put in direct sunlight. Roots should not be allowed to dry out at any time.
Uses: a multi-purpose plant in the home, which can be used alone or in groups.
Propagation: take cuttings a few inches long and insert five or six around the rim of a small pot filled with soil.

JAPANESE SEDGE

(*Carex morrowii variegata*)
Family Cyperaceae. A genus of about 2000 sedge- or grass-like herbs from marshes.
Habit: long, stiff evergreen leaves with white margins. Three-cornered stems rather than two dimensional.
Description: although of a different family, Carex is similar in many ways to the Acorus, looking like a variegated grass. Closer examination shows that the 'grass' blades are actually three-

Carex

Chlorophytum

cornered and they have a fine tooth edge which can cut the hand if carelessly drawn along them. Carex is really a water or bog plant and needs to have its roots constantly wet rather than moist. If grown in a low-sided pot the leaves will arch up and over to hide the container and look almost like a complete grass ball.
Needs: the roots of Carex must be kept wet at all times and it does no harm for the container to be stood in a cache pot with an inch of water in it. The plant is hardy so has no special need of warmth. An occasional feed will help growth but is not vital. This is a good plant to use on the verge of a small indoor pool where aquatic and marshy plants are grown.
Dangers: if the roots are allowed to dry out the grass-like foliage will turn brown and die, although it will probably regenerate itself if watered again before too much time has passed.
Uses: a waterside plant.
Propagation: bunches or clumps of the 'grass' can be pulled apart and planted individually in well-moistened peat.

SPIDER PLANT

(*Chlorophytum comosum*)
Family Liliaceae. A genus of about 40 species of grassy, evergreen perennials.
Habit: long green leaves with a central white stripe and a 60 cm (2 ft) scape bearing first tiny white flowers and then miniature plants with exposed roots.
Description: this is another grass-like plant, again easy to grow but not from the marsh. It is popular and widely grown largely because it is easy to look after and because propagation is simple and foolproof. Although the little flowers are modestly attractive they finish quickly and the main interest is in the long, arching scape bearing the tiny immature plantlet. The tips of the long leaves tend to turn brown after a time but this is usually a symptom of age and if unsightly the brown tips can be cut away completely or merely trimmed.
Needs: this is a fairly tolerant plant which grows easily under normal home conditions. Do not allow the soil to be too wet for long nor let it get too dry. Cool or warm conditions both suit except for extremes. A little humidity is helpful, for too dry air will lead to browning of leaf tips.
Uses: a good plant for a hanging basket or some other elevated position.
Propagation: simply peg into another pot one or more of the little plantlets and cut the scape when growth is seen.

KANGAROO VINE

(*Cissus antarctica*)
Family Vitaceae. A genus of about 200 species, mainly of climbing vines.
Habit: a natural climber with tendrils and medium-sized slightly toothed leaves.
Description: this is one of the best house plant climbers, needing no special treatment. It thrives in cold and warmth, in shade and direct light, taking draughts and other normal difficulties easily. Although it has tendrils these do not grasp hold of a wall, trellis or other support and it is necessary to train the many trails in the direction in which you wish them to travel. Although it is long-lived, some of the lower leaves will dry and drop after a few years, but the gaps are usually covered by new growth.
Needs: one of the easiest of house plants, the Kangaroo Vine will grow well in lightly shaded conditions and in widely differing temperatures. It will last well if left unwatered for a week or two and although it enjoys a certain amount of humidity, this need be no more than that provided by an opened window, rather than spraying.
Dangers: in winter if the air is allowed to become too dry, Cissus will sometimes attract red spider mite, a pest discouraged by providing a little humidity in the air.
Uses: a good climber for wall, doorway, or to act efficiently as a room divider.
Propagation: Cissus plants are easily grown from cuttings, which will root if placed in water.

Cissus

CROTON

(*Codiaeum variegatum pictum*)
Family Euphorbiaceae. A genus of about six evergreen shrubs mainly from Sri Lanka.
Habit: widely variable shrubs with vividly coloured leaves, smooth and shining, in most colours except blue.
Description: recent hybridization has resulted in stronger plants which will grow in the home for more than a few days. Today's specimens are still difficult but with care can be made to last for weeks if not months. The Croton is one of the most vividly-coloured of all plants, with multi-coloured foliage in many shapes with a shining, waxen surface. Leaves can be almost round, oval, oblong or long and strap-like. The colouring can be in the form of spots, splashes, streaks and sometimes even solid tones. Croton bleeds a milky juice when cut or damaged and this sap will stain clothing.
Needs: good light; a temperature of not less than about 16°C (61°F). This plant needs constant humidity and a regular spraying programme is advisable, although the provision of a moist cache pot will do much to satisfy requirements. Given extra humidity a Croton is less likely to drop its lower leaves while young.
Uses: a beautiful and very special plant for decorating the house.

Propagation: by cuttings at any time of the year, preferably woody rather than soft and using a rooting powder and a propagating case at about 21°C (70°F).

COLEUS

(*Coleus blumei*)
Family Labiatae. A genus of about 150 species, perennials, annuals and sub-shrubs from the tropics.
Habit: a perennial of about 30-45 cm (12-18 in) with soft, toothed leaves in many brilliant colours or mixtures.
Description: the Coleus is a familiar plant in home and garden, easily grown from seed or cuttings. It is vividly splashed with colour, sometimes solid, sometimes spotted, streaked, margined or dotted with red, orange, yellow or green. Colours are always brilliant in spite of the soft leaf texture. Racemes of white or purple flowers are produced but these are pinched out to keep the strength of the plant for the foliage. To keep this brilliant leaf colour it is essential that plants get as much light as possible, even direct sunlight, although this must mean that they are heavily watered and kept moist at the roots at all times.
Needs: Coleus require plenty of light if their brilliant leaf colours are to be maintained. They are soft, sappy plants and need a moist soil compost and regular feeding to keep them strong and vigorous. Temperatures should not be allowed to drop below about 10°C (50°F).
Dangers: the soft growth of Coleus is vulnerable to dryness at the roots and an arid atmosphere.
Uses: the brilliant colours of the foliage make Coleus particularly attractive when in groups.
Propagation: Coleus seed is easy to grow into good plants. Sow in late winter and pot on as plants grow. Cuttings may be taken at any time.

Codiaeum variegatum pictum, *popularly known as Croton, will last much longer without dropping its leaves if the temperature in the home is maintained at a steady level.*

35

FLAMING DRAGONTREE

(*Cordyline terminalis*)
Family Liliaceae. A genus of about 15 evergreen, palm-like shrubs and trees.
Habit: compact little shrub with spear-shaped leaves radiating from a central stem, with vivid green and red leaves.
Description: the name Flaming Dragontree indicates that this plant has vivid red leaves, sometimes mixed with dark green streaks. Leaves grow upright from the central stem on neat, short stalks. *C. terminalis* is slow-growing and difficult to keep.
Needs: temperatures should not drop lower than about 16°C (61°F) and plants should be kept in a light position out of all draughts. The soil should be slightly peaty and acid but well-drained and not wet.
Dangers: wet, soggy soil is probably the quickest way to kill a Cordyline, but hot sunshine is also harmful.
Uses: this is a versatile plant which will look well standing alone yet also fits happily into a mixed arrangement.
Propagation: seeds can be sown in a temperature of about 16-18°C (61-64°F) but stem cuttings at a slightly lower heat are quicker and more successful. Remember, first leaves are all green.

Cordyline australis *is a neat, easily grown plant in the home but in its native New Zealand it grows to 10 m (33 ft).*

EARTH STAR

(*Cryptanthus bromelioides tricolor*)
Family Bromeliaceae. A genus of 22 species of dwarf evergreen plants.
Habit: low-growing, starfish-shaped, pointed leaves striped white, green and pink. A fairly small plant.
Description: differs from most of the bromeliads by not having a central cup or vase, but the same spreading leaf pattern from the centre. Instead of arching outwards they lie flatter, with some of the central foliage more upright. As a soil 'hugger' Cryptanthus are particularly useful in bottle gardens and other plant arrangements for they make good ground cover and do not spread to invade other plants. There are several other species, such as *C. bivittatus,* with light and dark green stripes. All foliage is slightly waved at edges and all bear small and insignificant flowers.
Needs: like all bromeliads this is an easy and tolerant plant. It is one of the terrestrial type so the soil needs watering occasionally, but it should never be wet. Temperatures of about 18°C (65°F) are suitable and good light is necessary to maintain leaf colour.

Cordyline terminalis

Dangers: cold conditions and wet roots.
Uses: with a shallow rooting system Cryptanthus will grow well in a dish garden and because it is comparatively small and slow-growing it will have a long and useful life in a bottle garden.
Propagation: once again, like other bromeliads, the Cryptanthus will produce offsets rising from the soil and these can be removed and potted up.

roots is to be avoided and a certain amount of space is necessary.
Uses: if roots are confined in a pot the Cyperus will not grow quite as large as it might, but its chief use is for an indoor pool.
Propagation: by simply knocking the plant from its pot and teasing the clump of roots apart, one can make several new plants. The 'umbrella' at the top of the plant will also make roots if stood in water for a few days.

UMBRELLA GRASS

(*Cyperus alternifolius*)
Family Cyperaceae. A genus of some 550 species of waterside, marshy plants.
Habit: umbrella-like rosettes of leaves arch out from the top of a tall, thin, rigid stem, the centre holding a little tuft of insignificant greenish-brown flowers.
Description: this is a genuine water plant which likes best to stand in water rather than merely have wet soil. It will grow quite large, up to 2 m (6 ft) or so if in ideal conditions. There is a smaller species, *C. diffusus,* which grows only to about 60 cm (2 ft) in height.
Needs: plenty of water at all times. Plants should be fairly warm and in light shade.
Dangers: obviously dryness at the

Cyperus

Cryptanthus bromelioides tricolor

C. fosterianus

C. bivittatus

DUMB CANE

(*Dieffenbachia picta*)
Family Araceae. A genus of some 30 species of evergreen perennial plants.
Habit: large oblong leaves of 30 cm (12 in) or more from a central stem are marked with spots, blotches or streaks, mainly cream and green.
Description: the popular name comes from the fact that Dieffenbachia sap is poisonous and if any gets into the mouth it will cause the tongue to swell until one is unable to speak. Always wash hands carefully after handling the plant. *D. picta* has a number of varieties differing slightly in leaf colour.
Needs: warmth and humidity. In winter plants should never be cooler than 16°C (61°F) and should be plunged in a cache pot to give extra humidity. In winter give plenty of light and in summer keep the plant in light shade.
Dangers: keep out of all draughts. Hot sun will cause burning of the leaves and cold for long periods will kill it. Give less water in winter.
Uses: this can be a striking plant which should be given a special place.
Propagation: from cuttings (wash hands!) inserted in humidity in warm, moist peat.

D. p. Rudolph Roehrs

D. p. superba

Dieffenbachia picta exotica

Elegant indeed, this Dizygotheca will grow tall and stately, although it is almost impossible to stop some of the lower leaves dropping after a time.

FALSE ARALIA

(*Dizygotheca elegantissima*)
Family Araliaceae. A genus of about 17 species of evergreen trees and shrubs.
Habit: a small tree with elegant palmate leaves made up of 7-10 leaflets about 8 cm (3 in) long and about 1 cm ($\frac{1}{2}$ in) wide.
Description: young leaves are copper-coloured, gradually darkening to an almost black shade, and have regular saw-toothed edges. The little tree has a lacy, almost airy appearance

and in the home it will grow to 2 m (6 ft) or so in time, but as it ages the leaves become coarser and less attractive. On the whole older examples of the Dizygotheca are best thrown out to be replaced by younger and prettier plants.

Needs: Dizygotheca must have a certain amount of warmth, with a temperature of not less than about 16°C (61°F) at all times of the year. It must also be lightly shaded and must certainly not be exposed to hot sun. Humidity is not so vital as with some plants and watering should be carefully watched, the compost being maintained on the dry side. This is understandable when one realizes that the slender leaflets have very little space in which to exude moisture. The feeding programme should also err on the side of being light and gentle.

Dangers: cold conditions or too hot sun for too long a period. Wet roots will also cause considerable suffering.

Uses: young plants, tall, graceful and elegant, can make an effective focal point in a living room for a year or two.

Propagation: sow seeds 5 cm (2 in) apart in boxes of seed mixture in late winter in a temperature of about 21°C (70°F).

RIBBON PLANT

(*Dracaena sanderiana*)
Family Liliaceae. A genus of about 40 species of evergreen shrubs, palm-like and grown for foliage.

Habit: slender, pointed leaves in green and cream growing densely along a central upright stem, sometimes branching.

Description: there are a number of Dracaenas grown as house plants. All are distinguished by their many attractive leaves, usually green and white or gold, sometimes spotted, sometimes streaked or margined. Some grow quite large, although *D. sanderiana* is usually discarded after two or three years because it has lost its young beauty.

Needs: give plenty of light to encourage leaf coloration, but keep out of direct sun. *D. sanderiana* will tolerate a lower temperature than some other Dracaenas, but it should not be allowed to drop below about 10°C (50°F). Keep a little on the dry side in winter.

Dangers: root mealy bug is sometimes seen on this plant.

Uses: an attractive plant when young that fits equally well into a mixed arrangement or will stand on its own.

Propagation: new plants can be raised from basal shoots or from tip cuttings in a propagating case at about 21-24°C (70-75°F).

Dracaena sanderiana, *with its lovely green and white striped leaves is only one of the several species of Dracaena easily grown in the home.*

Invisible at first, the central stem of D. marginata becomes more apparent as the plant grows and as the lower leaves fall. The upright leaves at the top arch outwards as they mature.

MADAGASCAR DRAGON TREE

(*Dracaena marginata*)
Habit: tall-growing plant with slender pointed leaves arching from a central stem, medium-green with a red margin.
Description: this is said to be the easiest of the Dracaenas to grow in the home. It is an attractive, palm-like plant, best in its variegated form, known either as *D. m. tricolor* or *D. m. concinna,* with an additional cream stripe to the green and the red. As the plant grows it gradually drops its lower leaves and so eventually stands as a main stem or trunk holding at the top a tuft composed of the slim arching leaves.
Needs: good light is essential for the maintenance of the leaf colour, but direct sun should be avoided. There appears to be no method of forcing plants to hold on to their leaves instead of shedding them as they age. On the whole Dracaenas like to be kept just a little on the dry side.
Dangers: this is a comparatively easy plant, holding no special difficulties.
Uses: *D. marginata* makes an excellent display plant, to stand alone rather than in an arrangement.
Propagation: stems can be cut into pieces 7-10 cm (3-4 in) long and used as cuttings in a propagating case.

JAPANESE SPINDLE TREE

(*Euonymus japonicus*)
Family Celastraceae. A genus of nearly 200 species of evergreen and deciduous trees and shrubs.
Habit: an upright, bushy shrub with oval, glossy leaves, dark-green or in variegated form with white or yellow.
Description: *E. japonicus* is a plant which will grow well in a mild or well-protected garden and here it will produce green and white flowers in early summer. Indoors it is grown mainly in one of the variegated forms such as the popular *E. j. medio-pictus,* golden yellow, and *E. j. argenteo-variegatus,* silver. When young, plants should have their growing tips pinched out to encourage bushy growth and this practice can be continued through their lives.
Needs: plenty of light, even direct sun for comparatively short periods, will encourage good colour in the foliage. Conditions should be cool rather than warm and soil should always be moist. When growing strongly give regular but weak feeds.
Dangers: on the whole these are easy plants to grow, both indoors and out.
Uses: shown to best advantage as large specimens, particularly the golden form.
Propagation: by taking cuttings placed in a warm and humid propagating case.

Euphorbia

Euonymus japonicus *is an evergreen shrub which does well in the home if given cool conditions and as much indirect light as possible.*

POINSETTIA

(*Euphorbia pulcherrima*)
Family Euphorbiaceae. A genus of over 1000 species, annual and perennial herbs, trees, shrubs and succulents.

Habit: a deciduous shrub which grows from 60 cm (2 ft) to 3 m (10 ft) in height with oval or spear-shaped leaves and tiny yellow flowers above vermilion bracts, sometimes also white or pink.

Description: a popular winter plant since new and tougher strains of Poinsettia were bred in recent years. The tiny yellow flowers are unimportant compared with the vivid red bracts or modified leaves at the top of the plant.

Needs: with such vivid bract colour Poinsettia needs as much light as it can get and in winter can even stand directly in the sun. Temperature should be about 17°C (62°F). Although the roots should be kept moist they must never be too wet; let the soil dry out a little between the regular waterings.

Dangers: cold conditions; draughts; a polluted atmosphere; wet roots.

Uses: the Poinsettia is a winter or Christmas gift plant.

Propagation: cuttings root best in warm, moist conditions with frequent fine spraying of the leaves. Allow severed end to dry and treat with rooting powder before inserting.

TREE IVY

(*Fatshedera lizei*)
Family Araliaceae. A bigeneric hybrid of *Fatsia* and *Hedera*.

Habit: a trailer with dark-green palmate leaves 10-25 cm (4-10 in) wide, usually trained up a cane and grown as a climber.

Description: a particularly interesting plant because hybrids from two genera are very rare indeed. It makes a good house plant, attractive in appearance, quick to grow and more or less trouble free in the home. Although generally grown as a climber, it can also look attractive if allowed to sprawl along a shelf or other suitable surface. Trails will quickly reach to 3 m (10 ft) or more. Although the leaves appear to be tough and leathery, leaf shining products may cause considerable damage. Plain water and a soft sponge will clean the leaves efficiently and make them shine.

Needs: Fatshedera appears to enjoy normal home conditions. It should have good light but not direct sunlight and temperature should be much as we demand for ourselves. It should be watered regularly so that the root ball is kept moist but not allowed to become wet. An occasional light feed will help the plant to grow and stay in good health.

Dangers: there are no major problems.

Uses: suitable either as a climber or trailer. The uniform palmate leaves also make the plant interesting enough to be grown alone in a large pot.

Propagation: cuttings can be taken in summer of tip or side shoots and rooted in a soil mixture of half peat and half sharp sand. When roots have formed young plants can be potted up for use.

Fatshedera

CASTOR OIL PLANT

(*Fatsia japonica*)
Family Araliaceae. A genus of two species of evergreen shrubs.

Habit: an evergreen, erect shrub with large, green, palmate leaves, rich and glossy, 15-40 cm (6-16 in) wide.

Description: *Fatsia japonica*, sometimes known as *Aralia sieboldii* or *Aralia japonica*, also grows well outdoors in mild districts. There is a variegated form, *F. j. variegata*, with white markings on the leaves, sometimes difficult to obtain and perhaps rather more difficult to care for.

Needs: Fatsia is a plant which likes to be cool rather than hot and likes a dappled shade and moisture at the roots such as it would get in good garden soil. In the garden it will grow to 3-5 m (10-15 ft) tall and nearly as much wide and although it will not reach these proportions indoors, it can still make an imposing plant. Because it grows so strongly, it should receive regular feeding in addition to an annual repotting into a slightly larger pot with fresh, rich soil plus extra peat. Fatsia plants do not like hot, dry conditions indoors. They should be placed in a position where the temperature will not rise above 10-15°C (50-60°F) and where the air is fairly fresh and humid at most times.

Dangers: hot, dry or arid conditions.

Uses: The Fatsia can occupy considerable space when mature so it can be used to fill a corner or decorate a foyer.

Propagation: seeds can be sown in spring without special warmth and plants potted on when fit to handle. Alternatively, sucker shoots can be removed and treated as cuttings.

The variegated Fatshedera is perhaps a little more delicate than the plain green, but the variegated palmate leaves add interest and brightness to the plant.

Fatsia

The graceful Weeping Fig will grow into a tall tree if conditions are right, but this will take some years under most home conditions.

WEEPING FIG

(Ficus benjamina)
Habit: a tree which in the wild will grow tall and handsome but can be kept to more reasonable proportions in the home. Its name derives from its slightly weeping habit of growth.
Description: perhaps the most graceful of the tree-like figs, with its shining green leaves and slim, pendulous branches. It will grow quite large given good conditions but can be cut back to size and will quickly adapt itself after shedding a few lower leaves.
Needs: *F. benjamina* seems to need a slightly warmer home than other Ficus plants — about 15°C (60°F). It does best in good light and its roots should be allowed almost to dry out between waterings. The leaves, light-green and shining at first, turn darker as they mature on the graceful plant.
Dangers: hot sun; cold, wet roots.
Uses: a plant for larger rooms or for public places that can take advantage of the size.
Propagation: take cuttings of lateral shoots in early summer and place in pots of half peat, half perlite in a propagating case at 16-18°C (61-64°F).

MISTLETOE FIG

(Ficus diversifolia)
Habit: normally a small shrub in the home, with almost round leaves and many small berries, green to yellow in colour.
Description: the grey-green leaves of this fig are not particularly attractive and it is really the little berry-like fruits that have given the plant its popular name and its interest. This is a slow grower and although it will make a large shrub in its native land, it usually stays less than 1 m (3 ft) in height indoors. It is helpful to pinch out growing tips of laterals to keep the plant round and bushy.
Needs: a fairly easy plant to grow indoors. It likes a light situation and a constant temperature of about 16°C (61°F). Roots should be kept just moist at all times, no more.
Dangers: waterlogged soil. Wet roots will result in berries dropping. Too much heat or strong sunlight will turn the grey-green leaves brown.
Uses: an unusual shrub, not always easy to find, which has a certain curiosity value as a house plant.
Propagation: cuttings about 7 cm (3 in) long should be inserted in equal parts of peat and sand in a propagating case at a temperature of 16-18°C (61-64°F).

RUBBER PLANT

(*Ficus elastica decora*)

Habit: strongly-growing small tree with large, glossy, almost oblong dark green leaves uncurling from an orange-red sheath.

Description: there are now a number of forms of the familiar Rubber Plant. *F. e. decora* was an improvement on the original old *Ficus elastica* and there have been other improvements since, with greater tolerance, larger and glossier leaves and a number of new variegated forms. *F. e. robusta* is probably the best green form available today, and *F. e. schryveriana* the best variegated form. All rubber plants have large leaves which tend to become dusty. They should be cleaned regularly, using a soft sponge and tepid water, preferably rain water. Do not use chemical leaf shiners as they injure the texture of the leaves if they are applied too often.

Needs: all rubber plants prefer to be cool rather than hot, so try to keep them at about 10-15°C (50-60°F) and out of direct sun. Plants should be watered carefully, for the roots must be kept uniformly moist without being either wet or dry. Err on the side of dryness to be safe, but when watering make sure the whole of the root ball has been moistened.

Dangers: the greatest danger is too much water at the roots. Yellowing leaves which eventually drop off are a certain sign of over-watering.

Uses: either in an arrangement, when small, or as a decorative feature in its own right.

Propagation: by cuttings from lateral shoots, by leaf bud cuttings or by the more complex process of air layering.

Ficus diversifolia

Ficus elastica decora

FIDDLE LEAF FIG

(*Ficus lyrata*)
Habit: the large, glossy and slightly crinkled leaves are shaped roughly like the body of a violin, hence the name.
Description: *F. lyrata* is very much like the Rubber Plant except for the shape of the leaves and the fact that it is rather more difficult to grow well and for long. It is a strong grower and must have plenty of water and plant foods, but this also means that it quickly becomes pot bound and must be moved on to larger and larger pots. If held too long in too small a pot the lower leaves will turn yellow and drop off. It may be a little difficult to tell if this is happening because the main veins of *F. lyrata* are a paler green than the leaves, almost a yellow in colour.
Needs: this Ficus needs to be kept a little warmer than others and the temperature should not be allowed to drop below about 18-21°C (65-70°F). When in full growth it will need plenty of water and regular feeding, but in winter the water should be reduced and the feeds stopped until growth begins again in spring. Keep out of direct sun and make sure that the leaves are cleaned of dust.
Dangers: with such a vigorous grower it is necessary to watch the plant closely and not to let it stay too long in too small a pot.
Uses: a good specimen of *F. lyrata* will decorate a complete room.
Propagation: take cuttings 10-15 cm (4-6 in) long of lateral shoots and root them in a temperature of 21-24°C (70-75°F).

CREEPING FIG

(*Ficus pumila*)
Habit: a creeping plant with small green leaves on thin, wiry, black stems.
Description: this differs so much from other Ficus plants that it may be difficult to realize that it belongs to the same family. The pale green leaves are only 2 cm (1 in) or so long and they are produced in profusion on the wiry stems which trail from the pot. This is a good plant for a hanging basket but perhaps it is best in a plant arrangement where the trails can wind between other plants to form a veritable carpet of green. If the plants are plunged in moist peat or placed on a moist gravel bed, the little creeper will quickly cover the surface and put out new roots.
Needs: moist, humid conditions, some shade and protection from any direct sunlight. Plants should also be

Ficus lyrata

warm and out of all draughts, cold or hot. The soil of Creeping Fig must never be allowed to dry out or the leaves will quickly shrivel and die. It must have moist roots always.

Dangers: the greatest risk is dryness at the roots. However, do not saturate: if trails lie on moist peat or on moist gravel they will get the water they need. Spray daily in hot weather to keep plants in health.

Uses: the trailing stems will cover a moist surface or climb a wall if it can be moistened slightly so roots can hold.

Propagation: if grown on a moist surface this creeper will put out so many roots that pieces can merely be cut off as a complete plant.

Ficus pumila

Of the widely-ranging fig family Ficus radicans *is one of the most unusual and one of the most difficult. The white and green leaves are papery in texture and drop from the stems if the atmosphere is hotter and drier than it likes. Daily spraying is usually helpful.*

TRAILING FIG

(*Ficus radicans variegata*)

Habit: a creeping and trailing plant with small green and white leaves.

Description: *F. radicans variegata* is similar in some respects to *F. pumila* but is perhaps slightly more wiry and dry and certainly more difficult to grow for long periods in the home. It is very much happier in a humid greenhouse than in the comparatively arid conditions of the home. *F. radicans* is best grown in a bottle garden or terrarium, where it can enjoy its own microclimate of humidity. A danger here, however, is that the plant might enjoy these conditions so much that it makes rampant growth and so chokes itself and other plants.

Needs: warm, humid conditions with good light but no direct sun.

Dangers: dryness at the roots; sun; dry air; draughts; cold.

Uses: like *F. pumila*, *radicans* needs moist conditions and will do best if allowed to trail on some moist growing medium, or if sprayed frequently with tepid rain water.

Propagation: several short cuttings can be inserted in a pot of well-drained soil or peat and kept in a propagating case at about 16-18°C (61-64°F) until rooted, then moved to larger pots.

A delicate plant with paper-thin, red-veined leaves, Fittonia verschaffeltii *is a difficult plant to keep for long unless conditions are exactly right.*

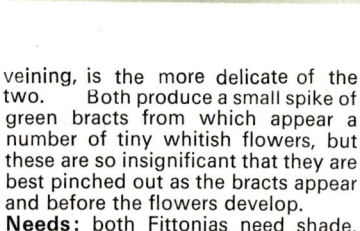

Fittonia argyroneura

veining, is the more delicate of the two. Both produce a small spike of green bracts from which appear a number of tiny whitish flowers, but these are so insignificant that they are best pinched out as the bracts appear and before the flowers develop.

Needs: both Fittonias need shade, warmth and humidity to a greater extent than is normally available outside a greenhouse. Temperatures should not drop below about 20°C (68°F) with high humidity. The protection of a bottle garden or terrarium is essential if plants are to be held in good condition.

Dangers: cold will kill plants within hours as will hot sun or even too strong daylight. Leaves will begin to shrivel if the potting soil dries out, but on the other hand this should be kept just a little drier in the winter than summer.

Uses: these are lovely little plants for growing in a terrarium or bottle garden, but often begin to straggle a little and should be pinched back if this is seen to be happening.

Propagation: stem cuttings will root fairly easily in a warm propagating case or plants can be divided from spring onwards.

SNAKESKIN PLANT

(*Fittonia argyroneura*)
Family Acanthaceae. A genus of three species of evergreen perennials with ornamental foliage, including *F. verschaffeltii*, the Red-veined Fittonia. From Peru.

Habit: small, low-growing with dull green leaves veined respectively in silver or white and a deep, striking red.

Description: two of the most beautifully foliaged plants in the house plant world. The leaves are about 8-10 cm (3-4 in) long and not quite so wide, as thin as tissue paper and so delicately veined that the plants have been given the popular name of Snakeskin Plant. Both *F. argyroneura* and *F. verschaffeltii* are exceptionally beautiful, although it is said that *F. argyroneura*, with the

PURPLE PASSION VINE

(*Gynura sarmentosa*)
Family Compositae. A genus of about 20 species of evergreen perennials but only two normally grown.
Habit: a trailing or creeping plant which will grow to 1 m (3 ft) or more in height, with attractive foliage and stems covered with fine purple hairs.
Description: *G. sarmentosa* is a little easier and perhaps more pleasing than *G. aurantiaca,* which has not the same trailing habit. Both have the same striking and attractive hairy surface so brilliant under different lights that plants have been named after velvet fabric. They produce yellow, daisy-like flowers which are said to have a grossly offensive smell, although in a ventilated room this is hardly noticeable. Both are strong growers and require repotting every year or replacing by fresh cuttings. The trails are not self-clinging and will need some support. Frequent pinching out of the growing tips will induce a more bushy type of plant. The trails can be used to some advantage if two or three plants are inserted among other types in a hanging basket.
Needs: plants should be kept warm, at a temperature of not less than about 16°C (61°F) and given as much light as possible in winter but some shade in summer, when more water and more humidity are needed.
Dangers: these are not really difficult plants so long as they receive some warmth and humidity and protection from direct sunlight and cold draughts.
Uses: place the plant in such a position that the light shines on the velvety leaves and stems to best effect.
Propagation: take 8 cm (3 in) cuttings of strong shoots in spring in a warm propagating case at 18-21°C (64-70°F).

Gynura sarmentosa

The beautiful soft leaves of Gynura sarmentosa *are covered with fine purple hairs.*

HEDERA

(*Hedera* species)

Most house plant ivies are developed from the common or English ivy, *Hedera helix*, an outdoor plant, which indicates that they prefer cool to hot conditions. Most, however, will adapt themselves to warmth just as they will adapt themselves when taken from the home and planted in the garden. In too warm a room leaves may tend to brown at the edges and perhaps even shrivel and drop. This will be due to attack by the red spider mite, prevalent where the atmosphere is dry and arid. Frequent spraying or the provision of more humidity will help to prevent it. If found, it can eventually be eradicated by spraying, particularly the undersides of the leaves, with a suitable pesticide.

Apart from this problem, ivies are extremely tolerant and easy plants to grow indoors. Some varieties can be kept small and compact by regularly pinching out the growing stems. Others can be encouraged to spread high and wide so that they cover a wall or grow into a dense pillar. If given a chance some will cling to a wall with adventitious roots along the stems and here they will do no real harm to the fabric of the wall, although when removed they will probably take some wallpaper with them.

There are all-green types, small- or large-leaved, and among the variegated forms there are those with white, cream, grey, yellow and gold leaves. Among those with variegated foliage are the large-leaved varieties of *H. canariensis*, the Canary Islands Ivy. These include *H. c. variegata*, also known as Gloire de Morengo — green, grey and white or cream; *maculata*, more mottled with its variegation, and the dark-green and yellow *H.* Goldleaf. There are many *Hedera helix* varieties with slightly smaller leaves in most cases. Chicago and Pittsburgh are two basic green varieties which can hardly be bettered. Variegated forms appear to be more popular indoors than the plain green and these include Glacier, with small leaves, green, grey and white; Adam and Little Diamond, again grey and white; *lutzii*, with marbled yellow and green. One of the prettiest ivy plants for the garden is the Jubilee or Gold Heart variety, brilliantly yellow and green, sometimes producing a leaf here and there of pure gold and another of soft green. Unfortunately this does not branch well indoors and for this reason is not nearly so effective in the home. *Digitata* has five finger-like lobes to leaves and *sagittaefolia* is arrow-shaped, five-lobed, with the centre one long.

Needs: ivies are easy indoors. Keep cool rather than warm and give plenty of light but not direct sun. Keep as humid as is convenient to you and spray your plants daily in hot, summer conditions. Keep roots moist but not wet, feed regularly but lightly and repot annually. Train plants the way you wish them to grow and if they grow too large for their situation, cut them back to half their length in spring. They soon recover.

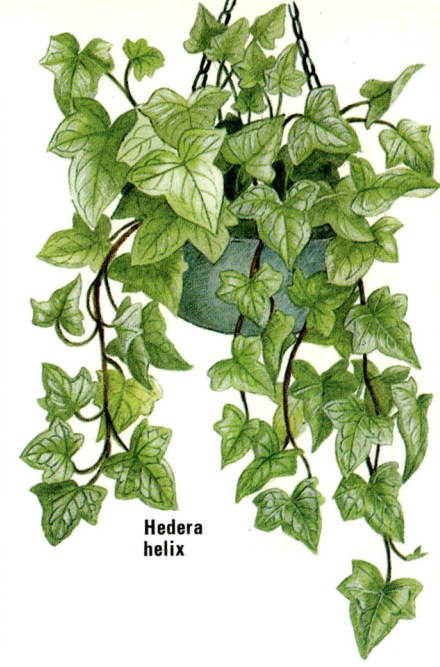

Dangers: hot, arid conditions, which often lead to attack by red spider mite.

Uses: plants can be grown to climb or to trail. Climbing plants should be clipped or tied unless you have no objection to the adventitious roots growing onto your walls, in which case trails will quickly make attractive patterns across walls and ceiling. It is usually best to grow ivies up a cane or trellis, for this way they can be controlled, pinched out and sprayed.

Propagation: cuttings root easily in peat, sand or plain water without the necessity of a propagating case.

Hedera helix

Hedera helix *Jubilee is probably more attractive grown outdoors than in the home, for it does not branch as freely as most ivies. The green and the gold, however, are more vivid here than in other ivies.*

51

MIND YOUR OWN BUSINESS

(*Helxine soleirolii*)
Family Urticaceae. A single species. A creeping, half-hardy, perennial foliage plant from Corsica.
Habit: small round leaves, glossy green, on long, prostrate, slender pink stems.
Description: a dense ground cover plant with tiny green leaves. One or two small pieces in a pot of peaty soil mixture will grow quickly and become a mound of foliage before spilling over the sides to cover the surface nearby. They may become untidy if left to grow for too long, in which case it is an easy matter to pluck pieces and root them in a new pot.
Needs: keep cool rather than warm and in light shade during the summer, when plenty of water should be given. Less water is required in winter. A temperature of not less than about 7°C (45°F) should be maintained.
Dangers: dryness at the roots or too arid an atmosphere will brown the tiny leaves, but these may be hidden in time by new growth which is always coming.
Uses: mainly a curiosity plant but it makes a good ground cover for a group of plants.
Propagation: pluck a few pieces of Helxine from an old plant and push them into a pot of moist peat.

PARASOL PLANT

(*Heptapleurum arboricola*)
Family Araliaceae. A genus of 200 species of evergreen tropical trees and shrubs.
Habit: a quick-growing, single-trunked tree with 'umbrella' or 'parasol' spoke leaflets growing at the end of a stalk.
Description: also called *Schefflera venulosa erystrastachys*, *H. arboricola* makes an elegant tree-like plant which can be allowed to grow tall or may have its growing tip pinched out to give it a more bushy habit of growth. This is a quick grower and one has to decide quickly whether to have a tall plant or one that is more bushy. It can be cut down strongly in late spring and will quickly make new growth from this point. Young plants will soon fill their pots with roots and will need repotting annually until they have occupied 25 cm (10 in) pots. Their growth will slow down if allowed to stay and given a regular feed with a proprietary food.
Needs: plenty of good light but no direct sun; moderately warm conditions; some degree of humidity; clean air.

Heptapleurum

Dangers: no real difficulties here.
Uses: this is a graceful but dignified plant that should stand alone in a well-favoured position in the home.
Propagation: by sowing seed in spring at about 21-24°C (70-75°F) or taking stem cuttings in a propagating case.

POLKA DOT PLANT

(*Hypoëstes sanguinolenta*)
Family Acanthaceae. A genus of more than 40 species of evergreen shrubs or perennial herbs from South Africa and the tropics.
Habit: a herb up to 30 cm (12 in) tall, with pointed oblong leaves, deep-green, splashed and dotted with pink spots.
Description: an advantage of Hypoëstes is that it is easily raised from seed, so it is possible to have many plants at little cost. The leaves are somewhat sparse, although a regular pinching out programme will help to make the plant thicker and more bushy. The pale purple flowers produced are small and insignificant and should be pinched out as they begin to appear in order to retain greater strength for the important foliage.

Hypoëstes

The tiny-leaved Helxine soleirolii will spread to form a carpet of leaves. Spray it with tepid water if the room is dry.

Needs: these are not difficult plants to grow indoors. Because of the leaf coloration they should be placed where they will get good light but little or no sun. Keep fairly warm but not hot. Roots should be kept in a moist state at all times and not allowed to dry out or leaves will shrivel and turn brown before falling. A certain amount of humidity is helpful. Draughts, hot or cold, should be avoided.
Dangers: dry roots; draughts; cold. Scale insects may attack the undersides of leaves.
Uses: the most striking way to display this plant is to grow several together in a large bowl placed in a light position.
Propagation: easily grown from seed. It is equally easy to grow plants from cuttings in spring in a warm propagator.

BLOOD LEAF

(*Iresine herbstii*)
Family Amaranthaceae. A genus of about 20 species of erect herbs or sub-shrubs.
Habit: a small, shrubby plant grown only for its vivid red or carmine leaves.
Description: a most unusual plant which is grown indoors and in outdoor bedding schemes after all danger of frost has passed. The foliage and stems are a superb, almost translucent red. The greenish-white flowers are inconspicuous and should be removed. Plants tend to become somewhat 'leggy' and straggly unless they are kept pinched out to encourage a bushy habit. It also helps bushy growth if plants are given a light situation although direct sun will burn the delicate foliage. Cool conditions suit them rather than too warm and even in winter they should not be in temperatures of more than about 13°C (55°F).
Needs: plenty of water in warm months, less during winter; cool rather than hot conditions; good light but not direct sunlight for long periods.
Dangers: hot, arid conditions; lack of water at the roots; a drawn and sparse appearance through lack of pinching out growing tips; frost.
Uses: a good plant either to stand alone or to use in a mixed plant arrangement. Always a dramatic contrast to all other plants which may be grown in the home.
Propagation: from cuttings at almost all times of the year except midwinter. As young plants look best it is wise to have a constant succession.

The brilliant red foliage of the Iresine makes it an attractive plant. Place it where the light can shine through the leaves, but keep out of direct sun.

PRAYER PLANT

(*Maranta leuconeura*)
Family Marantaceae. A genus of 14 species of perennial herbs.
Habit: small, low-growing plants with delicately marked oval leaves about 15 cm (6 in) long, growing on short stems.
Description: the two main species are *M. l. erythrophilla,* a dark olive-green with central yellow-green strip and vivid red veins, and *M. l. kercho-veana,* with a paler green leaf and a series of darker splashes up each side. The name comes from the way the plant folds its leaves together at night, like hands in prayer. Another name, Rabbit Tracks, comes from the shape of the blotches on the leaves.
Needs: Maranta needs good light to keep its foliage colour, but no direct sun, even for brief periods. Marantas like to be modestly warm, about 18°C (65°F), and should have a little local humidity, which can be provided by an efficient cache pot.
Dangers: sunlight; cold; arid conditions.
Uses: these are beautiful plants which should be placed to give greatest pleasure.
Propagation: by cuttings at any time placed in a heated propagating case.

SWISS CHEESE PLANT
(*Monstera deliciosa*)
Family Araceae. A genus of some 50 species of evergreen climbers.

Monstera

Habit: an unusual plant characterized by its large green serrated leaves, and its climbing habit.
Description: this well-known climber will grow to the ceiling and produce huge 1 m (3 ft) leaves, if given the treatment it likes. Better to grow the identical but smaller version, *M. pertusa*, which has the same serrated and holed leaves and aerial roots.
Needs: warm, moderately humid conditions and a regular watering and feeding programme. Pot on annually until the optimum size has been reached, because the best leaf holing and serration is then encouraged and maintained. Lead aerial roots down into the pot.
Dangers: wet, waterlogged roots; too small a pot; too large a plant.
Uses: a dramatic climber that will grow to the ceiling. Not for small rooms.
Propagation: generally by seed sown in boxes in a warm propagating case. Young plants have entire leaves at first. In agreeable conditions, serrations appear after the first year.

Among the most beautiful of house plants, Marantas always look attractive because of their lovely leaves. They do not make a strong root system, so they need potting on only every second or third year using a soil mixture that is light and open in texture. Feed lightly but regularly in summer. In winter cut down on water and food.

BIRD'S NEST

(*Neoregelia carolinae tricolor*)
Family Bromeliaceae. A genus of about 40 species of evergreen perennials.

Habit: spiny, strap-like rosettes of leaves around a central cup or vase which contains the insignificant flowers.

Description: one of the more vividly-coloured bromeliads. The deep-green and cream leaves can reach a spread of up to 60 cm (2 ft) and when the little purple flowers appear in the cup, the centre of the rosette 'blushes' to a vivid scarlet. The flowers may not live long but the leaf colour remains for months.

Needs: keep the plant reasonably warm and the central cup or vase filled with water. Do not apply fertilizer with water to the central cup as this will cause staining. Instead, pour a little diluted liquid fertilizer onto the soil once a month in spring and summer.

Dangers: overwatering, which causes root rot.

Uses: an engaging and attractive plant, preferably to stand alone.

Propagation: by division of offsets. Knock the plant out and with a sharp knife cut away and pot each new plant.

BLUSHING BROMELIAD

(*Nidularium innocentii*)
Family Bromeliaceae. A genus of some 22 species of epiphytic herbs forming leaf rosettes.

Habit: the spiny linear leaves are a dark-green above, purple beneath.

Description: typical central vase and spreading leaves, perhaps just a little taller than most bromeliads (45 cm, 18 in) and forming not quite so definite a cup for the tiny greenish-white flowers that appear in the centre of the rosette as it turns brilliant red. The cup must be kept filled with water at all times and the soil should be kept just moist. Plants should be in a light situation and will not mind direct sun for a limited period each day, and a little humidity may be applied. Temperatures should not normally be lower than about 16°C (61°F).

Needs: few. See that conditions are not too cold or too hot, dry and arid, and that the cup is kept filled.

Dangers: overwatering of the soil.

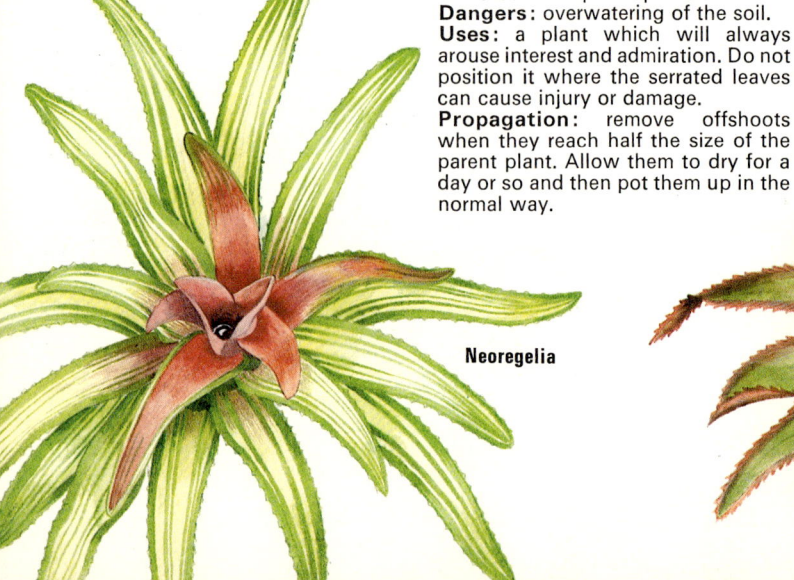

Uses: a plant which will always arouse interest and admiration. Do not position it where the serrated leaves can cause injury or damage.

Propagation: remove offshoots when they reach half the size of the parent plant. Allow them to dry for a day or so and then pot them up in the normal way.

Neoregelia

Pandanus in the home seldom grows to more than about 60-90 cm (2-3 ft).

SCREW PINE

(*Pandanus veitchii*)
Family Pandanaceae. A genus of about 600 species of tropical evergreen trees and shrubs.
Habit: tall-growing, with 60 cm (2 ft) slim, pointed leaves, green and white striped, drooping from a central stem.
Description: the common name comes from the screw-like or helical manner in which the leaves spiral around the stem, the word 'pine' coming from pineapple because of a superficial resemblance. The plant has sharply-spined leaves and needs handling with considerable care. This is a plant which resembles a palm and could almost be a bromeliad, but is neither. However, it has the same characteristics of tolerance and ease of cultivation as the other families. Good light, average temperatures and rather less water than normal are the modest demands of Pandanus.
Needs: it is helpful to grow Pandanus in a plunge or cache pot to give a little added humidity. Otherwise try to water sparingly and make sure in winter that no water collects in the spaces between the leaves. Empty out if necessary.
Dangers: overwatering can lead to a form of root rot.
Uses: a fine plant that may in time demand considerable space.
Propagation: a mature plant will send up offshoots from the soil around the stem base and these can be removed, potted up and placed in a propagator. Young plants also form on the trunk of more mature plants.

Nidularium

DARK NETTING

(*Pellionia pulchra*)
Family Urticaceae. A genus of about 15 species of herbs.

Habit: a small creeping plant with small leaves in various shades of green, brown and grey depending on the plant and the quantity of light it has been receiving. Young plants are usually a fairly clear green and silver or white. The fleshy stem bearing the many 2-3 cm (1 in) leaves will continually root at the nodes as it crawls on any moist surface. After a time when the plant becomes rather lank and straggly, it is easy enough to break off sections and root them merely by lying them on a surface of moist peat or sand.

Needs: a temperature of about 15°C (60°F) but will give better value for greater warmth. There should be some humidity and a lightly shaded position, although a better light at certain times of the day will result in a better coloration of the foliage.

Dangers: dryness; cold, arid atmospheres.

Uses: to cover soil surfaces where plants are grouped on a tray or in a bowl, or in a hanging basket.

Propagation: the fleshy stems make roots as they crawl on a moist surface. Take cuttings from these and pot them up.

Pellionia

WATERMELON PEPEROMIA

(*Peperomia argyreia, P. sandersii*)

Habit: small — 15-23 cm (6-9 in) tall — and wide with smooth, thick leaves up to 10 cm (4 in) long.

Description: the leaves, borne on stalks which are usually pinkish-red, are round to oval and thick and chunky. The almost metallic silver background cover is overlaid with very dark-green bands radiating from the stalk tip along the major veins.

Needs: plenty of light in winter but some shading in spring and summer; a temperature not less than 16°C (61°F) and a humid atmosphere. Plants can well do with daily spraying in summer and should have the protection of a cache pot. Winter watering should be very light.

Dangers: overwatering; low temperatures.

Uses: most Peperomias are versatile plants and this is no exception. It will go well alone or mixed in a group.

Propagation: by leaf cuttings. Either use the whole leaf or cut into four, inserting cut ends into a peat-sand mixture.

The unusual leaf markings of Peperomia argyreia *follow and echo the outline of the thick and solid leaves.*

EMERALD RIPPLE

(*Peperomia caperata*)
Habit: small, 2½ cm (1 in) heart-shaped corrugated or crinkled leaves, green, on pink stalks, rise from a central stem.
Description: leaves here are smaller and so crinkled or corrugated that one would expect to feel the roughness. They are dark green and radiate from a central, low, thick, pink stem. This is a neat and pleasant little plant which is easy to grow and develops only slowly so that it takes some time to become straggly and untidy. There is a variegated form but this is rather more difficult to cultivate under normal home conditions.
Needs: moist roots but not wet; some warmth; good light; some humidity.
Dangers: dry roots; arid atmosphere; low temperatures for long periods.
Uses: a good little plant for a community or an arrangement. Suits bottle gardens.
Propagation: take leaf cuttings with a portion of stalk which should be buried in the peat-perlite growing medium.

Peperomia magnoliaefolia

Ridged and wrinkled leaves of Peperomia caperata *contrast dramatically with the white 'rat-tail' flower spikes which rise above them.*

DESERT PRIVET

(*Peperomia magnoliaefolia*)
Habit: low-growing, much-branched and shrub-like plant with chunky, oval, glossy leaves about 5 cm (2 in) long.
Description: the variegated form is usually the one that is seen and sold. This has foliage of a light cream when immature and this gradually changes to pale green so that a mature plant will have many green and cream leaves borne on red or red-spotted stems. All the Peperomias have a rather shallow root system and wild examples are more or less epiphytic. This suggests that they do not require large pots to grow in and that their roots should be kept slightly on the dry side.
Needs: plenty of water in summer, much less in winter; a humid atmosphere; some shade during summer but as much good light as possible in winter days.
Dangers: dry roots; arid atmosphere.
Uses: a good decorative plant for use alone.
Propagation: take stem cuttings about 7-8 cm (3 in) long and insert in a well-drained medium such as peat and perlite.

Philodendron bipinnatifidum

TREE PHILODENDRON

(*Philodendron bipinnatifidum*)
Habit: a low-growing plant with large green leaves spreading on long stems.
Description: leaves are like a large triangle, up to 60 cm (2 ft) long, with several deep incisions on each side. These leaves grow outwards from a central point so that a whole mature plant can stretch for some 1½ m (4-5 ft). The leaves uncurl prettily, first a pale and glistening green and then darker and firmer. The tendency is for the leaves to droop with their own weight rather than stand upright, except when immature, so the plant is really one which suits a hanging basket or a pedestal which is free-standing rather than placed against a wall.
Needs: this is an easy plant to grow where there is space enough. It likes plenty of water when growing fast but must never get soggy. Temperatures do not appear to matter too much as long as they are normal for the home. Light is not over-important and although some humidity is enjoyed it is not vital.
Dangers: dryness or wetness at the roots.
Uses: a spectacular plant best grown high so leaves can droop.
Propagation: plants are best grown from seed.

ELEPHANT'S EAR

(*Philodendron tuxla*)
Habit: a strong-growing climber with long, slim, pointed green leaves.
Description: the shiny green leaves are carried on stout stems and are up to 20 cm (8 in) long. So strong and heavy is the growth htat it is essential to give it good support. This is a plant that can well do with a strong stake well wrapped with sphagnum moss, kept in a moist condition, so that the aerial roots can cling and grow to this and gain support. The plant will grow up to 2 m (6 ft) tall. If aerial roots grow downwards try to lead them into the pot soil and do not cut them away unless there are too many.
Needs: some warmth; some humidity; generous watering in summer and less in winter; a lightly shaded situation.
Dangers: over-watering; a cold situation or one where the sun shines too strongly.
Uses: a striking plant, it can be grown up a good support to display its long arrow leaves effectively.

Dangers: overwatering; dryness at roots.
Uses: a versatile climber that can be kept to a convenient size and will look well or can be allowed to grow almost rampant and cover a wall or ceiling. It will grow almost anywhere in the house where there is a little light.
Propagation: by tip cuttings with a mature leaf, or pieces of stem with two or three joints, in warm conditions.

The long, narrow, shining green leaves of Philodendron tuxla *are long-lived and highly spectacular.*

Propagation: by tip cuttings taken with a leaf in late spring and inserted in a peat mixture at about 21-24°C (70-75°F).

SWEETHEART PLANT

(*Philodendron scandens*)
Habit: a strong-growing climber with green, heart-shaped leaves about 10 cm (4 in) long and clinging aerial roots.
Description: a tolerant, easy to grow climber which will live for years in the home, constantly adding to the length of its several long trails, each of which will grow to 6-7 m (20-25 ft) or more if this can be accommodated. The growing tips can be pinched out and the plant grown as a smaller, bushier type, in which case the aerial roots can be led down to the pot. If grown in trailing form the roots will cling to a wall or will grow quite eagerly into a mossed cane.
Needs: this is one of the easiest house plants to grow. As long as the home is moderately warm, given moderate light, water and food, the plant will thrive for years.

Philodendron scandens

The blend of green and brown gives an almost golden tone to the softly wrinkled leaves of Pilea mollis, *an attractive and easy plant for the home.*

Pilea cadierei

ALUMINIUM PLANT

(*Pilea cadierei*)
Family Urticaceae. A genus of some 400 species of evergreen perennials.
Habit: oblong oval leaves about 7-8 cm (3 in) long and half as wide, dark-green with regular silvery markings.
Description: a member of the nettle family of which the leaves are vaguely reminiscent. This Pilea has been almost completely replaced with a smaller, neater, easier form, *P. c. nana*, which is the one usually found in shops. Both plants should have the growing tips pinched out regularly to keep them in good shape.
Needs: *P. cadierei* will tolerate poor light, although not a really dark situation. In winter give it as much light as is available and a temperature of not less than about 10-13°C (50-55°F). Give plenty of water in summer.
Dangers: never let this plant dry out. Keep it just moist in winter.
Uses: *P. c. nana* looks well either in a group or standing by itself, its leaves shining out in a rather shaded corner.
Propagation: by stem cuttings in a peat-sand mixture in warmth in late spring.

MOON VALLEY PLANT

(*Pilea mollis*)
Habit: a creeping herb with deeply quilted green leaves overlaid with brown.
Description: leaves are a little larger than those of *P. cadierei* and quite different in texture, being soft and almost hairy in appearance. Some insignificant greenish-brown flowers sometimes appear low on *P. mollis* but these are best removed, as they have no particular interest.
Needs: a fairly easy plant, asking only

for a certain amount of warmth, good light — but not too much — and moist roots at all times, not too wet.
Dangers: extremes of all kinds will not be tolerated by this plant, even for brief periods.
Uses: this is another useful plant for the home as it will mix well with other plants yet give an interesting impression on its own.
Propagation: by stem cuttings taken in early summer. Push 8 cm (3 in) pieces in around the rim of a pot of peat and sand.

SWEDISH IVY

(*Plectranthus oertendahlii*)
Family Labiatae. A genus of 250 evergreens, mainly perennials and sub-shrubs.
Habit: a prostrate, creeping, foliage plant with 5 cm (2 in) round leaves having silvery vein markings.
Description: although there are many species in this genus, only two or three are normally available in commerce. The most important of these is *P. oertendahlii* and its variegated form, both of which have soft and almost hairy leaves. This is one of the best examples of a house plant, for it is attractive in appearance, easy to grow, making no special demands, long-lasting and versatile in its performance. Besides its pleasant foliage, it produces terminal panicles of pale pinkish-purple flowers in summer, which can either be enjoyed or pinched out to increase foliage strength and thickness.
Needs: some warmth; good light but not sun; plenty of water in summer, less in winter; regular light feeding.
Dangers: plants should not be allowed to become dry during the summer or they will quickly become flaccid and drop their leaves.
Uses: Plectranthus can be kept small and neat by pinching out growing tips constantly. Let it trail from a pedestal or hanging basket so that the drooping stems, 1 m (3 ft) or more in length, can hang beautifully. These long trails should not be allowed to grow too long or their weight will fracture the main stem.
Propagation: almost any portion of stem will root easily at almost any time of the year and in almost any medium from peat, sand and perlite to plain water.

Plectranthus forms a low bush with many green crenated leaves having a clearly marked cream margin.

Rheo

BOAT LILY

(*Rhoeo discolor*)
Family Commeliniaceae. A genus containing one species only, an evergreen perennial.
Habit: a rosette of fleshy, dark-green, spear-shaped leaves with purple undersides, up to 30 cm (12 in) in length.
Description: the leaves radiate upwards and outwards from a central thick, stocky stem or trunk and at the joint is produced the little boat-like involucre which holds the tiny white flowers. It is not always an easy plant to grow, demanding a rather high temperature and very careful watering.
Needs: a lightly shaded position is necessary and at no time should it be placed in direct sunlight. Roots should be moist at all times but never either too dry or wet. Temperatures should not be lower than about 18°C (65°F) summer or winter and preferably rather higher. A regular feeding programme will help to keep these plants in good condition.
Dangers: almost any serious deviation from the set methods of looking after the Rhoeo is likely to cause trouble.
Uses: this plant is really more of a curiosity than a decoration and it is the little boat-like flower holder that is the main source of interest.
Propagation: by cuttings of basal shoots in mild heat or by seeds sown in spring.

GRAPE IVY

(*Rhoicissus rhomboidea*)
Family Vitaceae. A genus of about eight species of evergreen shrubby climbers.
Habit: a vine with many dark-green leaves, it clings by hairy tendrils.
Description: this is not a flamboyant plant but one of the most useful because of its lack of demands and its strength and versatility. As a climber it is usually bought trained to a short cane, but it will quickly outgrow this and may require further support. It will grow up a tall cane, a trellis or any other means of support. It will suffer polluted air, low temperatures, lack of light and lack of humidity, although of course it will do better under more beneficial conditions. It can sometimes become rather dusty and may even harbour house pests such as spiders and woodlice if left ungroomed for too long.
Needs: plenty of water in summer, less in winter; light feeding when growing strongly. An occasional spray will refresh and encourage dry foliage. Try to give some ventilation when the weather is particularly hot and dry.
Dangers: too dry an atmosphere can lead to attack by red spider mite. Direct sun can burn the foliage.
Uses: a splendid plant to cover a wall or to create a division between parts of the house or a single room.
Propagation: cuttings 7-8 cm (3 in) long of laterals can be taken in spring or sections of main stem with two or more nodes.

MOTHER-IN-LAW'S TONGUE

(*Sansevieria trifasciata laurentii*)
Family Liliaceae. A genus of 60 species of perennials.
Habit: thick, stiff, sword-like leaves growing upright and up to about 1 m (3 ft) tall, green with mottled grey transverse bands and yellow margins.
Description: *S. t. laurentii* is the plant most usually seen. Less frequently seen are the lower-growing *S. hahnii* and its more attractive golden form. Some are said to be slow-growing, but given the right treatment all will reproduce themselves by offsets and fill the pot with growth in a year or two. Mature Sansevierias may produce tiny greenish-white flowers in summer.
Needs: Sansevierias are semi-succulent and will accept full sun for a time. They should be kept almost dry in winter but given water in summer to encourage the growth of offsets. They must never be waterlogged nor must they be over-fed.

Rhoicissus

Sansevieria hahnii is the less familiar of the two main Sansevierias. It has shorter, broader leaves but is equally easy to grow and demands just as little attention of any kind.

Sansevieria trifasciata laurentii

Sansevieria trifasciata *in an attractive pot-et-fleur arrangement.*

STRAWBERRY GERANIUM

(*Saxifraga sarmentosa*)
Family Saxifragaceae. A genus of 370 species of small hardy and half-hardy annuals and perennials.
Habit: height and spread about 30 cm (12 in) with many long, red, thread-like stolons carrying baby plants.
Description: Saxifraga has long, hair-like stolons or runners which hang down for up to 1 m (3 ft) or so, each bearing at the end a young plant which can be pegged down into a pot of soil and will grow. In summer small white flowers appear, but even these take second place to the stolons and young plants. Put the plant where these stolons can hang and be noticed, preferably on a pedestal rather than in a hanging basket.
Needs: although the root ball should be kept moist, the surface of the growing medium should be dry enough to let the stolons move freely. Some warmth is necessary and plenty of good light. It makes no particular demands for humidity so long as the root ball is moist and the atmosphere is not arid.

Dangers: over-watering. Temperatures should not be allowed to drop below about 10°C (50°F).
Uses: make the plant appear more interesting by allowing offshoots to grow and create a thick forest.
Propagation: by offsets is easiest. These can be separated and potted. Leaf cuttings will not produce the characteristic yellow striped edge.

Dangers: cold; too wet or too dry soil.
Uses: the plant must be placed high so that the interesting stolons can be seen to hang over the edge.
Propagation: the little plants at the end of the stolons should be placed on a pot of suitable soil and pegged in place until actively growing, when the stolon can be cut.

UMBRELLA PLANT

(*Schefflera actinophylla*)
Family Araliaceae. A genus of some 200 evergreen tropical trees and shrubs.
Habit: a tall, single-stemmed, tree-like plant with glossy green leaves divided into three or five oblong-ovate leaflets.
Description: an elegant and graceful small tree. When young, the shiny green leaves are divided into three leaflets, when mature into five, radiating like the spokes of an umbrella.
Needs: some warmth; good light in winter, no sun in summer; moisture at the roots; some protection against hot air and cold draughts. Tall plants must have a large pot.
Dangers: the only dangers are extremes of heat and cold, dryness and lack of light, none of which are likely under normal conditions in the average home.
Uses: this is a space-filling plant which is graceful enough for the home but particularly useful in public places.
Propagation: by seed in late winter in a warm and humid propagating case.

The elegant grace of a Schefflera belies the strength of the plant. It makes no demands for any special treatment or care.

Saxifraga

67

Scindapsus aureus *is an attractive climbing plant and can also be encouraged to trail gracefully from a hanging basket.*

DEVIL'S IVY

(*Scindapsus aureus*)
Family Araceae. A genus of 40 species of evergreen climbers.
Habit: a tall climber with variegated heart-shaped leaves.
Description: this Scindapsus is very much like *Philodendron scandens* except that the leaves are larger, fleshier and variegated. It is one of the most tolerant of house plants. There are cultivars Marble Queen, with foliage flecked and marbled with white, and Golden Queen, where the leaves are almost completely yellow.

S. aureus will climb well with its own aerial roots if given a moss-bound cane or similar support. Alternatively, trails will wind and travel attractively between the pots of a large group arranged in a peat or moist gravel tray. Plants must have a degree of humidity and warmth or they will turn black at the leaf tips and gradually die inwards. They like to be a little on the moist side in summer, much drier in winter and should never have to live in a temperature lower than about 13-16°C (55-61°F), summer or winter.
Needs: warmth, humidity and plenty of light, even sunlight in cold winter days, though never in the summer. A regular spraying programme, using clean, tepid rain water, will be helpful to the plants as will applications of dilute fertilizer.
Dangers: cold; dry, arid conditions. Plants tend to bruise if handled too roughly or if trails are allowed to brush against furniture or walls.
Uses: this delicate and beautiful climber is well worth growing in a light spot where it can be trained to climb a sturdy cane well wrapped in moist sphagnum moss.
Propagation: cuttings of tip growth or basal shoots will root in peat and sand in a propagating case at about 21-24°C (70-75°F) with plenty of humidity.

The foliage of S. aureus *Marble Queen is flecked and marbled with white.*

CAPE IVY

(*Senecio macroglossus variegatus*)
Family Compositae. A genus of about 3000 species, world-wide.
Habit: a tall, evergreen climber with ivy-like leaves and small daisy-like flowers.
Description: like a rather more dainty ivy with glossy leaves and a few unexpected flowers. It makes a good climber but only to its limits — little more than 1 m (3 ft) — after which the plant tends to straggle and lose its looks. But it roots so easily that frequent replacement is no problem. Senecios are more tolerant of hot, dry situations than ivies and are consequently considerably easier.
Needs: this is not a difficult plant, asking no more than average temperatures, good light and enough moisture to keep the roots cool.
Dangers: a preventive spray of insecticide is recommended against greenfly.
Uses: a good climber that will crawl up almost any support.
Propagation: an astonishingly easy plant to grow from a cutting. It will root in almost any medium in any of the warmer months of the year and at a speed which ensures a plentiful replacement supply.

GERMAN IVY

(*Senecio mikanoides*)
Habit: an all-green climber with ivy-like leaves, tolerant of dry conditions and with a speedy habit of growth.
Description: this plant appears to be rather tougher and coarser than *S. macroglossus*, largely because it is all green. It is a quick and strong grower and will make a taller plant. It also makes a good trailer until the growth begins to coarsen and straggle, and will produce yellow flowers.
Needs: like Cape Ivy, an easy plant to grow as long as basic needs are met.
Dangers: greenfly attack, or extremes in the environment.
Uses: this plant will either climb or trail, so can be trained up a support such as a mossed pole or can be allowed to hang from some suspended container. The dark-green leaves achieve a powerful visual effect against a light background.
Propagation: cuttings will root quite easily at most times of the year.

Senecio macroglossus

Senecio mikanoides

AFRICAN HEMP

(*Sparmannia africana*)
Family Tiliaceae. A genus of seven species of evergreen flowering shrubs.
Habit: a quick-growing shrub with lime-green, hairy leaves and white flowers.
Description: this plant is such a quick grower that some authorities suggest it should be cultivated as an annual and replaced each year. Others recommend potting on in fresh soil for no more than three years. It is easily replaced from cuttings. The soft green leaves, hairy on both sides, are attractive in their own right, but the plant also produces large white flowers with purple-tipped stamens. Although tender, the plant prefers cool rather than hot conditions and enjoys ventilation.
Needs: the soft green leaves will remain turgid only if the root ball is kept moist at all times, but no special humidity is required, so long as the air is not too dry. Temperatures can go as low as about 7°C (45°F).
Dangers: hot sun directly on the plant will scorch the leaves, but it should have good light for the sake of the $2\frac{1}{2}$ cm (1 in) flowers.
Uses: foliage and flowers make this plant attractive as a flower arrangement so long as it is kept in fresh condition.
Propagation: by cuttings 8-10 cm (3-4 in) long taken from young growths in spring and inserted in a peat-sand mixture at a temperature of about 16°C (61°F).

Sparmannia

STROMANTHE

(*Stromanthe amabilis*)
Family Marantaceae. A genus of about 15 species of herbaceous perennials with rhizomatous roots.
Habit: a low-growing foliage plant with curious and attractive greyish marks radiating from the central vein of the oval, blue-grey leaves, 10-15 cm (4-6 in) long.
Description: this interesting plant, very similar to some of the Marantas and Calatheas, can be a good one for the home, if well looked after, for this is one of the plants that is highly allergic to sunlight. It must not be in deep shade because of the leaf coloration, but it must definitely be protected against strong sunlight. Stromanthe is also fussy about its soil which should be light and well-drained, yet capable of holding moisture, which suggests a peat-based mixture. The leaves are striking

and appear to be far more delicate than they actually are. They will grow very thickly and after a time a pot will become thick with growth, making a mound of delicately marked exotic foliage.
Needs: apart from its aversion to the sun, Stromanthe makes few demands. It likes moderate warmth, moist roots and the humidity it can gain from a cache pot. Do not let the soil dry out or get too wet.
Dangers: direct sun for more than just a few minutes at a time will do great harm to this tender plant.
Uses: the delicacy of the leaf patterns makes a plant of special interest.
Propagation: stem cuttings taken with one or two leaves attached will root in peat in a temperature of about 20°C (68°F).

The beautiful and delicate foliage of Stromanthe should be kept away from strong sunlight. If given moderate warmth and humidity, this plant will produce a mound of foliage.

GOOSE FOOT PLANT

(*Syngonium podophyllum*)
Family Araceae. A genus of about 14 species of climbing shrubs from South America.
Habit: creeping or climbing aroids with leaves about 15 cm (6 in) long shaped like an arrowhead or a goose foot.
Description: this is perhaps a little smaller than most of the aroids and more gentle and delicate. It has the same climbing or creeping habit. Leaves are normally a dark-green with lighter markings. The Syngonium will make a fair-sized plant if required, but it is best grown up a mossed stick to a height of up to 1 m (3 ft) or so.

Needs: like all the other aroids the Syngonium likes a little shade, some warmth and humidity and a regular feed when growing well. In the winter plants should be kept almost dry and protected against cold.
Dangers: a dry, arid atmosphere will cause leaves to brown at the edges, as will strong direct sunlight. The roots must never be allowed to dry out but should not be too wet.
Uses: the Syngonium can be a striking plant in the home if it is trained to grow up a mossed pole and show off its leaves. Make sure that the moss is kept moist at all times, preferably by spraying once a day during summer months, and the plant will put out its roots, grasp hold and pull itself upwards.
Propagation: new plants are best grown from cuttings, which will root quickly and easily in a warm propagating case.

CHESTNUT VINE

(*Tetrastigma voinierianum*)
Family Vitaceae. A genus of about 40 species of evergreen or deciduous climbers.

Syngonium

Syngonium Green Gold

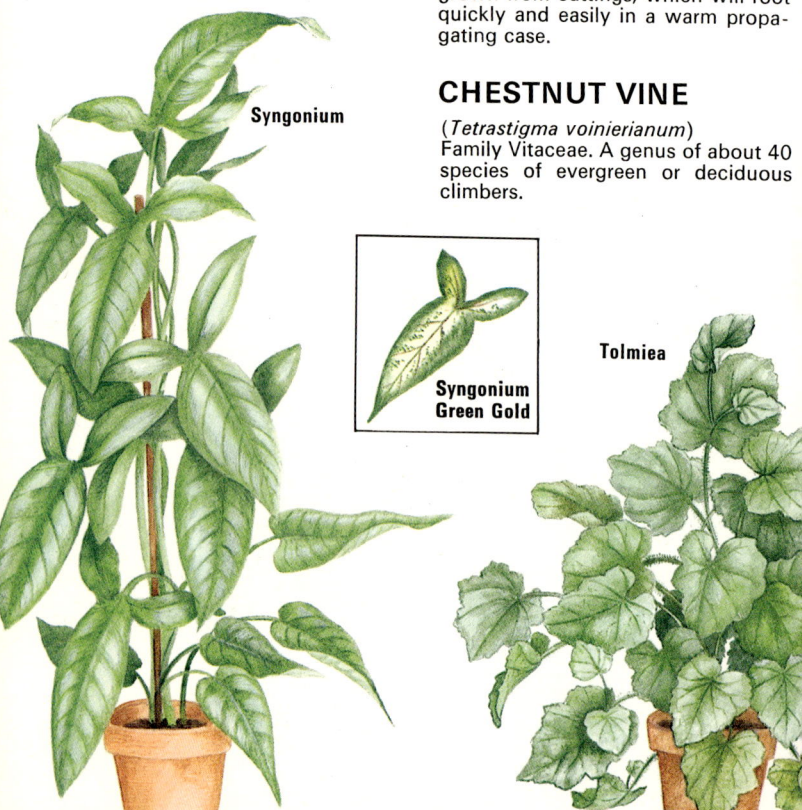

Tolmiea

Habit: a vigorous vine with large leaves, downy beneath, and strong tendrils with which it clings to supports.

Description: this is probably the most rampant of all house plants and one that should not be grown by anyone without space to spare. The popular name comes from the shape of the leaves, but unlike those of the Chestnut they are thick and downy beneath and glossy on the surface. The thick stems carrying the growth are brittle when young and easily snap off at a touch, although new growth is made immediately at this point. It is best to train the several growing stems up trellis or a long, strong rope.

Needs: large quantities of water and fertilizers, but only when growth is active. Tetrastigma is uncertain about seasons and will sometimes grow rapidly in winter and stay static in summer. Temperature should be between 15-21°C (60-70°F) through the year.

Dangers: it is easy to break a stem unknowingly and then water heavily because the plant seems to droop. So examine it carefully for any damage. Do not water excessively when the stems are not putting out extravagant growth.

Uses: this rampant climber must have a staircase or a lofty hall in which to grow in the home.

Propagation: stem cuttings will root without much trouble in a warm situation. Choose firm and woody growth rather than the softer and sappy tissues.

Tetrastigma

PICK-A-BACK PLANT

(*Tolmiea menziesii*)
Family Saxifragaceae. A genus of a single species of herbaceous perennial.

Habit: many-leaved stems growing from a creeping rhizome, with a bud at the top of the leaf stalk producing new young plants on the leaves of the old.

Description: one of the very few house plants which is completely hardy and will grow happily in the garden, dying down in winter but growing again in spring. Young plantlets grow on top of the leaves. When removed and placed on a pot of soil, they will grow without further treatment.

Needs: as an outdoor, hardy plant Tolmiea prefers cool conditions to hot and will grow happily at 10°C (50°F).

Dangers: if temperatures are too high or air too dry, attack from red spider mite can be expected, so spray with rain water as a preventive measure.

Uses: mainly a curiosity plant, although the light-green foliage is very attractive. It is better maintained as a young plant, since it will become loose and untidy in appearance when older.

Propagation: new plants are easy enough to grow, so replace old ones frequently. Merely pick a young plant from the surface of a leaf and place it in a pot of soil.

SILVERY INCH PLANT

(*Tradescantia* species)
Family Commelinaceae. A genus of about 50 species of low perennial herbs.
Habit: creeping perennials with leaves about 4 cm (1½ in) long, the three-petalled flowers triangular in basic outline.
Description: the variegated types of Tradescantia — silver, white or gold — are much more interesting than the plain green, so if any plain green shoots appear they should be pinched out at once or they may take over. It is a pity that the houseplant Tradescantias achieved such wide fame so quickly. They are so easy to grow and to propagate that they are to be seen everywhere, usually brown, stringy, meagre and sad. They need only a little water and plant food now and again and pinching out to keep them stocky and well-coloured. Among the rather less usual types is *T. sillamontana*, a very special type with soft grey-green leaves and stems thickly covered with fine, white, silky hairs. Few of those most frequently seen are named varieties and many differ or even change colours according to the light or other attentions they may have received.

An interesting shape, the Yucca is gaining in popularity as a house plant.

Needs: some warmth, some moisture, some food, some humidity and plenty of light.
Dangers: probably the greatest danger is neglect, for they are so easy to grow that they are sometimes forgotten.
Uses: only well-grown plants can stand on their own, otherwise best in an arrangement with others.
Propagation: trail ends that have been pinched out can be pushed into the parent pot or a new one to grow easily.

Tradescantia

T. fluminensis tricolor

T.f. variegata

SPINELESS YUCCA

(*Yucca elephantipes*)
Family Liliaceae. A genus of about 40 species of evergreen trees and

shrubs, mainly from South America.
Habit: a palm-like tree rising from a swollen based stem, with long, narrow, glossy-green leaves.
Description: until comparatively recently Yuccas were grown only in gardens with a Mediterranean-type climate or in the greenhouse. New cultivars are hardier and are usually sold as small green plants with slim arching leaves from a central stem or trunk. The leaves of most garden species have a dangerously sharp terminal spike.
Needs: Yuccas need good light, even direct sun for short periods and a warm atmosphere. Well-drained soil should be kept just moist at all times.
Dangers: too wet a soil and too cool conditions can lead to fungus attack.
Uses: a dramatic plant, preferably for display where space is available.
Propagation: normally from root or stem cuttings, but some species will produce offsets which can be separated.

Zebrina

The leaves of Zebrina pendula, *striped silver with purple tints.*

WANDERING JEW

(*Zebrina pendula*)
Family Commelinaceae. A genus of four species of trailing perennials.
Habit: a trailer with oval leaves about 7-8 cm (3 in) long, silver and green above and a rich, shining purple beneath.
Description: similar and allied to the Tradescantias, but with more vivid colours: deep greens, metallic silvers, royal purples. The best-known form of *Zebrina pendula* today is Quadricolor, with the upper leaf striped white and rose-purple and the underside deep purple. Small purple flowers are produced in little clusters during the summer.
Needs: once again the Zebrinas need much the same treatment as the Tradescantias: some warmth, plenty of water in summer and less in winter, regular feeding and good light. Keep plants out of direct sun in summer but give them as much as they can get in winter to keep good colour.
Dangers: neglect; drought; overgrowth.

Uses: good for a hanging basket or pedestal, where they can get good light and can show off both leaf sides.
Propagation: take cuttings at any time of the year and root them in pots of any good soil mixture without extra heat.

FERNS

Ferns bear no flowers and in their natural state propagate themselves by means of minute spores, usually carried on the underside of leaves. They can be large or small and in spite of their dainty and delicate appearance they are tougher than you think, so should be grown in the home under cool, lightly shaded and moist conditions.

MAIDENHAIR FERN

(*Adiantum capillus-veneris*)
Family Polypodiaceae with more than 200 species of tropical and temperate ferns.
Habit: small, one-sided segments of foliage and no distinct midrib.
Description: small, fan-shaped leaves borne on slender, black, wiry stems.
Needs: all Maidenhair Ferns are tender and frost will damage or kill them. They like a little more light than most other ferns, but never direct sun, and a warm humid atmosphere. Soil should be rich, light and exceptionally well-drained.
Dangers: frost or too cool conditions; too hot and dry an atmosphere.
Uses: ideal for fern cases and the humid conservatory.
Propagation: by division or by spores, which are comparatively easy to germinate.

ASPARAGUS FERN

(*Asparagus plumosus*)
Not a real fern. Family Liliaceae with more than 100 species, many varieties.
Habit: evergreen climber.
Description: fine, feathery, filamented leaves on smooth stems. Produces up to four white flowers at the end of twigs, followed by purple-black berries.
Needs: light shade; cool, airy atmosphere; plenty of moisture at the roots; regular feeding.
Dangers: hot sunlight, stuffy atmosphere.
Uses: the long climbing stems can be trained to grow up string or trellis. Fronds popular with florists in the makeup of posies and buttonholes.
Propagation: by seed in spring or by dividing roots at almost any season.

Asparagus

Adiantum

SPLEENWORT

(*Asplenium bulbiferum*)
Family Aspleniaceae, with more than 600 species from all parts of the world.
Habit: evergreen fern with large, lanceolate, soft-green fronds.
Description: grows up to 60 cm (2 ft) tall with a spread of about 1 m (3 ft). The finely-cut fronds bear tiny

Asplenium nidus

The Mother Spleenwort, Asplenium bulbiferum, *is a most unusual fern which propagates itself by means of little bulbs on its fronds.*

bulbils which gradually weigh them down to touch the soil surface where they will begin to grow and propagate themselves.
Needs: a moist atmosphere but a well-drained soil. Some warmth and humidity are helpful to grow an attractive plant.
Dangers: cold, over-wet roots; sun.
Uses: a decorative house plant, which can easily be propagated.
Propagation: by bulbils growing on its fronds, which should be picked off when three or four leaves have developed, and potted up in a light, well-drained soil mixture and kept warm and humid.

BIRD'S NEST FERN

(*Asplenium nidus*)
From tropical Asia and Pacific islands.
Habit: large lanceolate leaves growing from a central rosette, newest growth coming from the centre.
Description: grown in a pot in the home or in a greenhouse the long, glossy-green, almost waxen leaves will grow up to 130 cm (4 ft) long and between 8 and 20 cm (3-8 in) wide.
Needs: warmth, light shade and humidity are necessary to grow a large and healthy plant. Growth is generally slow and plants will not as a rule need repotting more frequently than once every three years or so. Leaves may attract dust and should be washed occasionally. Also spray plants to increase their local humidity.
Dangers: cold; changeable conditions; hot sun. Leaves tend to become brown at the edges if they are carelessly handled or brushed against.
Uses: large decorative pot plant.
Propagation: by spores, a difficult operation best left to experts.

MALE FERN

(*Dryopteris filix-mas*)
Family Aspidiaceae, a genus of about 150 species, world-wide, with many varieties, most of them hardy.
Habit: typical wild fern.
Description: parallel, horizontal fronds, growing small or as large as 2 m (6 ft). Evergreen when pot-grown or in any sheltered place, easily grown under almost all circumstances.
Needs: some shade and protection from frosts; a light sandy loam and plenty of water at the roots.
Dangers: under normal conditions one of the easiest and most tolerant of ferns, indoors or out.
Uses: an easy and decorative fern.
Propagation: spores germinate easily in midsummer. Division also effective.

There are several dwarf forms of the Male Fern, Dryopteris filix-mas.

HOLLY FERN

(*Cyrtomium falcatum*)
Family Polypodiaceae, about 10 species from Asia.
Habit: nearly-hardy evergreen ferns.
Description: stiff, arching, evergreen fronds, glossy, green, tufted and with drooping extremities, firm and leathery. Fronds are shaped a little like holly leaves without the sharp spines.
Needs: the Holly Fern is one of the tougher examples of this breed and will live happily in a house or in a room where the temperature drops as low as 7°C (45°F). When cold, pots should be kept almost dry, but in summer they should be given ample water. Plants are quick growers.
Dangers: the Holly Fern will accept cooler conditions than many, but not frost. Keep out of summer sun.
Uses: this is one of the most useful of evergreen ferns because of the tolerant habit of growth, the speed at which the plant grows, the glossy and handsome appearance and strong, leathery growth.
Propagation: spores should be sown in pans kept moist by standing in water.

BOSTON FERN

(*Nephrolepis exaltata*)
Family Oleandraceae, with 30 species.
Habit: typical free-growing fern.
Description: evergreen, up to 60 cm (2 ft) tall, spreading, bright- to pale-green, many-fronded and free-growing. *N. e. bostoniensis* has wide fronds and a quick growing habit.
Needs: keep fairly cool, away from sun and draughts. Soil should be kept moist at all times but well-drained.
Dangers: scale insects can sometimes attack the Boston Fern; control

The Boston Fern, Nephrolepis exaltata, *makes an attractive display in a hanging basket.*

by spraying with malathion. Draughts are death to these plants, so keep them in a cool (10°C 50°F) and protected place.
Uses: the Boston Fern is particularly suited to growing as a hanging basket plant in a place such as a greenhouse or conservatory, where it will make a ball of feathery green.
Propagation: by stolons, separated and potted in a peat-sand mixture.

dwarf forms, has fronds branched and crested.
Needs: keep cool and give good light without direct sunlight. In summer it can go outdoors for a few months in a lightly-shaded and protected situation and where it can be kept lightly moistened at all times.
Dangers: too strong sunlight. Lack of sharp drainage will cause root rot.
Uses: this is a good multi-purpose fern that can be used in many parts of the home and can even be planted out in the garden or placed on the terrace.
Propagation: by spores or by division in late winter or early spring.

HART'S TONGUE FERN
(*Phyllitis scolopendrium*)
Family Aspleniaceae, with only eight species and several varieties.
Habit: evergreen, strap-shaped entire fronds, sometimes forked.
Description: will grow to 60 cm (2 ft) in height and will spread to some 50 cm (20 in). Suitable both for indoor and garden use. Variety *crispum* has crimped and waved frond margins; *cristatum*, with several

Phyllitis

STAG'S HORN FERN

(*Platycerium bifurcatum*)
Family Polypodiaceae, a genus of 17 species of epiphytic ferns.
Habit: evergreen fern with two types of fronds, barren and fertile.
Description: long, grey-green and almost furry fertile fronds branch out at their ends to resemble the horns of a stag. The almost round sterile or mantle fronds serve to anchor the fern to its tree and are brown and papery when mature.
Needs: some warmth; shade; moisture.
Dangers: over-watering when pot-grown.
Uses: highly decorative, the Stag's Horn Fern looks best growing on an elevated piece of wood or bark. Knock the plant from its pot and line the root ball with moist sphagnum moss. Secure with plastic-covered wire, then tie this in turn onto the wood. Keep the roots just moist at all times.
Propagation: by spores, a difficult and lengthy process, or by division.

The Stag's Horn Fern grown indoors has none of the impact of the larger, more vigorous plant growing, epiphytic, on a tree in its native land.

Platycerium

The Ribbon or Brake Fern, Pteris cretica *is probably the most popular fern for the home. It is attractive, easy and long-lived. It has several forms.*

RIBBON FERN

(*Pteris cretica*)
Family Pteridaceae, a genus of 250 species.
Habit: upright stems bearing horizontal or drooping ribbon fronds.
Description: light-green pinnate fronds with strap- or ribbon-shaped pinnae. The variety *albolineata* has a white line down the centre of each pinna. *Wimsettii* is the name given to the heavily-crested types frequently seen in commercial decorations of stores and salesrooms.
Needs: fairly cool conditions, light shade, plenty of water in summer and very little in winter.
Dangers: fairly trouble-free.
Uses: an easy to grow, long-lasting, inexpensive form of decoration, particularly of public places and commercial establishments.
Propagation: by sowing of spores at a temperature of 13°C (55°F) in spring. Spores germinate so easily that extra plants will often appear unwanted in a heated greenhouse.

SELAGINELLA

(*Selaginella kraussiana*)
Family Selaginellaceae, a genus of more than 700 species of mainly small, evergreen plants closely allied to the ferns.
Habit: ground-covering, moss-like.
Description: mainly small and low-growing, vividly green, with tiny leaves so thick that the plants look almost like a moss. *S. kraussiana* is a little more spreading than others of

Selaginella

the genus and its trails will grow to 30 cm (12 in) or so. Varieties include *aurea,* with golden foliage, and *variegata,* a variegated form.
Needs: warmth (16°C or 61°F) and moist roots in humid conditions.
Dangers: cold; dryness at the roots.
Uses: the Selaginellas are particularly attractive when grown with larger ferns in a terrarium or bottle garden, situations in which they also thrive.
Propagation: by cuttings. A propagating case is essential, for the cuttings are so small that they will dry out without the humidity provided by this equipment.

PALMS

There is something a little nostalgic, even romantic, about palms, yet they are of great practical and economic value. They provide food and drink, roofing surfacings, ropes, oils, waxes and many other materials. Those that we can successfully grow in our homes are few in number but are surprisingly easy to cultivate and slow-growing enough to have a life of many years. Unfortunately this is a reason for their general scarcity and hence their comparative high cost. Some species can be grown from seed in the home.

Cocos

Phoenix roebelinii, *a relative of the Date Palm* (Phoenix dactylifera), *comes from India. It is more tender and slower growing than its relative.*

COCONUT PALM

(*Cocos weddeliana*)
Family Palmae; a genus of only one species.
Habit: arching, pinnate leaves of many slender, dark-green leaflets.
Description: a small, graceful palm for the home, only about 30 cm (12 in) high and wide in its early stages. It will grow to 2 m (6 ft) or so but may take 20 years to do this. Slender and graceful leaflets hang from the strong main stems.
Needs: warmth; ventilation; correct watering. Temperature should never be allowed to drop below about 16°C (61°F) in winter or below about 21°C (70°F) in summer. Plants should have plenty of water and be lightly shaded during the summer; little water and more light in the winter. Feed fortnightly during summer.
Dangers: this is a somewhat touchy plant that requires constant watching, for a little too much sun or water can cause it to sulk and then to die.
Uses: one of the most graceful of the palms, excellent for indoor decoration.
Propagation: by seed sown in late winter in high temperature and humidity.

SAGO PALM

(*Cycas revoluta*)
Family Cycadaceae. A genus of eight variable species of tropical evergreen perennials.
Habit: trunk cylindrical, sometimes rounded, ball-shaped, bearing at the top several stems with rigid, arching leaves composed of many leaflets with a midrib but no lateral veins.
Description: this is a member of the most ancient and primitive family of plants, now found only in tropical America, Australia, Africa and some tropical islands. In its native lands it will grow to about 2 m (6 ft) and bear leaves about 60 cm (2 ft) long.
Needs: good drainage; warm, humid air.
Dangers: cold, wet, soggy roots.
Uses: as decoration in an ornamental greenhouse or conservatory, or can be brought indoors for temporary enjoyment.
Propagation: can be grown from seeds or from suckers which sometimes appear.

The distinctive arching leaves and cylindrical trunk of the Sago Palm.

KENTIA

(*Kentia forsteriana, Howea forsteriana*)
Family Palmae, one of the two species from the Lord Howe Islands, hence the name.
Habit: dark-green pinnate leaves with drooping linear-lanceolate leaflets.
Description: one of the most familiar of the indoor palms. Will grow to 3 m (10 ft) or more in suitable conditions.
Needs: plenty of water in summer and a winter temperature of not less than 13°C (55°F). Shade from full sun in summer and give best possible light in winter. Kentias are quicker growing than most palms and have a longer life.
Dangers: dryness in summer; wet roots in winter; sudden changes of temperature.
Uses: Kentias are ideal for the corner of a room or for a hallway.
Propagation: seeds are large and can be handled individually. Sow on the surface of peat-filled pans in a temperature of no lower than 27°C (81°F). When they have germinated, pot into 7 cm (3 in) pots and grow in slightly cooler conditions.

Kentia

PARLOUR PALM

(*Neanthe bella*)
Family Palmae, with this as the only species.
Habit: dainty miniature palm tree.
Description: this is one of the easiest of the indoor palms, small, graceful and attractive with fairly wide leaflets. Unfortunately these grow coarse as the plant ages, so grow young plants for home decoration.
Needs: a tolerant plant, Neanthe will grow at lower temperatures and with lower humidity than that required by most palms.
Dangers: the growing medium must be well drained, otherwise wet roots will mean brown leaf tips.
Uses: a pretty little palm, easy to handle and highly decorative.
Propagation: seeds sown in peat beds with a high temperature (about 27°C, 81°F) and high humidity.

DATE PALM

(*Phoenix dactylifera*)
Family Palmae; a genus of some 17 species.
Habit: a slow-growing, graceful palm.
Description: good specimens have not only a graceful growth pattern but a pretty silvery sheen on the slender leaflets. This is the genuine Date Palm, which can be grown from a date stone.
Needs: this palm is unusual in needing lower growing temperatures than most palms, 7-10°C (45-50°F) will suffice. If the summer temperature gets higher than about 18-21°C (64-70°F) the room should be ventilated to give cooler conditions. Soil must be well drained and as the roots grow thickly an annual repotting is advised.
Dangers: cold, wet soil.
Uses: the date palm itself is a curiosity, a fun plant for a child, although growth is generally too slow for children.
Propagation: seeds may be sown in late winter and germinated in a temperature no lower than 18-21°C (64-70°F), in darkness and with some humidity. Shoots appear in about two months.

Neanthe

Phoenix

FLOWERING PLANTS

For those who seek living colour in their homes there are many flowering house plants, although they are obviously not in flower the whole year through. They range from familiar favourites such as Chrysanthemums to strange and exotic plants with even stranger flowers, such as Billbergia and Vriesia.

Abutilon

FLOWERING MAPLE

(*Abutilon striatum thompsonii*)
Family Malvaceae. A genus of about 90 species.
Habit: half-hardy herbs and shrubs with foliage like maple leaves.
Description: dark-green leaves mottled with yellow, and masses of orange-red flowers hanging down like little bells. Will grow quite large indoors and can be trained to cover a wall or climb a trellis.
Needs: temperatures no higher than about 10°C (50°F). While growing strongly plants should be given plenty of water and regular feeding, but in winter should be allowed to stay almost dry. In autumn, after flowering, stems can be cut back severely to encourage plenty of strong growth for the next flowering season.
Dangers: dryness at the roots: make sure the whole of the root ball is kept moist during the growing season and spray the foliage occasionally to increase humidity.
Uses: this is more a plant for the garden room or conservatory, for it needs space to look its best.
Propagation: sow seed in spring to raise plants with new colours, or take cuttings.

HOT WATER PLANT

(*Achimenes* hybrids)
Family Gesneriaceae, a genus of about 30 species from tropical America.

The vivid flowers of Achimenes hybrids can be white, yellow, pink, red, purple or blue.

Habit: herbaceous perennials with trumpet flowers in many strong and vivid colours.
Description: a small plant growing no taller than about 30 cm (12 in) and

often with so many flowers that the foliage is almost hidden behind them. The common name comes from the practice of plunging dormant tubercles in hot water before they are planted in late winter so as to speed development of the young plants.

Needs: a light situation and moderately warm conditions at about 16°C (60°F). The soil in the pot or hanging basket should be kept moist while plants are growing well in the summer and a regular feeding programme should be instituted. When growth begins to die down in autumn watering should be reduced until the soil is bone dry. The rhizomes can then be stored, ready for spring.

Dangers: if the atmosphere is kept too dry there is danger of attack by red spider mite.

Uses: as a summer pot plant for the light window and for bright hanging baskets.

Propagation: several methods are used: seed sown in early spring, rhizomes divided, leaf and stem cuttings taken.

GREEK VASE PLANT

(*Aechmea rhodocyanea, A. fasciata*)
Family Bromeliaceae, a large family of tropical American epiphytic and terrestrial plants.

Habit: large, grey-green, strap-like leaves growing in the form of a rosette to make a central vase or cup which holds water.

Description: the tooth-edged leaves are covered with a mealy down. From the centre of the vase a single stem arises which bears a spiky head of pink bracts in which nestle the tiny blue flowers. These fade but the attractive bracts remain almost as bright as flowers for many months.

Needs: bromeliads are tolerant of a wide range of temperatures, accepting both light and shade. The central cup or vase should always be kept filled with water and the soil always allowed to remain almost dry.

Dangers: wet soil leads to root rot and a dry vase will dehydrate an entire plant.

Uses: an easy and decorative plant for all parts of the home, usually better on its own than in a group.

Propagation: by offsets. These can be cut away with some roots attached and planted in a separate pot.

FLAMINGO FLOWER

(*Anthurium scherzerianum*)
Family Araceae. A genus of about 500 species of tropical American perennials.

Aechmea

Anthurium

Habit: typical cylindrical spadix above a bract-like spathe, sometimes large, often vividly-coloured and waxy.
Description: spear-shaped, dark-green leaves reach to about 60 cm (2 ft) on their short stems and surround rounder, bright-red spathes which each bear an orange-red spiralled spadix as long as 10 cm (4 in).
Needs: not an easy plant to grow well or for long. It needs good light and high humidity, so plunge the plant in a cache pot and spray frequently. Use a peaty soil mixture and water with rainwater. In winter keep rather drier and do not allow the temperature to drop lower than 16°C (61°F).
Dangers: dry air; dry roots; low humidity; low temperatures; too much lime in the soil.
Uses: Anthurium makes an attractive and long-lasting decorative plant in the home, suitable for any well-lit situation, warm and free of draughts.
Propagation: plants can be grown from seed. Sow in a light, open, peaty soil in a propagating case with a temperature no lower than 24°C (75°F).

ZEBRA PLANT

(*Aphelandra squarrosa louisae*)
Family Acanthaceae. A genus of about 60 evergreen shrubs from tropical America.
Habit: erect-growing shrubby plant with large, white-veined lanceolate leaves.
Description: the common name comes from the strong white markings on the dark-green leaves. Equally interesting are the yellow 'cockscombs' of red-tinged bracts which top the plants and last from three to six weeks.
Needs: not always an easy plant to grow indoors for long periods, as it needs careful attention. The vigorous root system demands constant feeding and must never be allowed to become dry at any time.
Dangers: Aphelandra will drop its leaves and quickly die if the roots are allowed to dry out even for a brief time. It will not flourish unless fed regularly with a mild fertilizer. It will fail to flower if in poor light, in a draught or in too cool a situation.
Uses: a striking and decorative plant, Aphelandra will outlast cut flowers.
Propagation: take cuttings in a propagator in a temperature of about 21°C (70°F).

The glossy, dark-green leaves of Aphelandra contrast beautifully with the bright yellow bracts.

AZALEA

(*Azalea indica, Rhododendron simsii*)
Family Ericaceae, with many species and many varieties. Mainly from China, Tibet and the Himalayas.
Habit: a small, woody shrub with small, tough, dark-green leaves and many blooms.
Description: the Azalea that we know is made to bloom artificially. Plants are kept small and compact and roots are trimmed to fit them into small pots. A good plant will have several flowers open and will be showing many fat buds ready to bloom.

Azalea

Needs: the most important need is a great deal of water and the plant must be able to send up a constant supply of nourishing sap to the many leaves and flowers. It is not enough merely to water Azalea as often as once a day: it must be well soaked by placing the pot in a bucket of water until all the air bubbles have ceased to rise from the soil surface. Cool conditions are better than hot, but no cooler than 10°C (50°F). A light spray of rainwater daily is good.
Dangers: dry roots will quickly kill the plant, as will strong, direct sunshine.
Uses: a splendid gift plant.
Propagation: a specialist task. With care it is possible to keep a plant in a cool and shaded place in the garden from one year to another, avoiding all frosts.

Although B. semperflorens *will be killed outdoors by frosts, they will flourish indoors through the winter if kept warm, moist, draught-free and in good light.*

BEGONIA

(*Begonia* species)
Family Begoniaceae, a genus of 350 herbs, shrubs and climbers from many parts of the world and highly developed by hybridists.
Habit: widely differing according to type, but generally recognizable by the lop-sided, roughly triangular leaves.
Description: there are four major groups of Begonia. The bulbous group includes the famous Gloire de Lorraine race of winter flowering plants. Tuberous Begonias are many

and include the Grandiflora varieties with large flowers and the Multiflora types with small single blooms. All are summer flowering. The group of rhizomatous Begonias includes the *B. rex* foliage plants.

The final group, fibrous-rooted, includes among many others the well-known *B. semperflorens,* which will flower for most of the year.

Needs: the greatest need of flowering Begonias is humidity, so all should be plunged in a cache pot where the insulating material is kept moist at all times.

Dangers: Begonias dislike being wet at the roots, so let them become almost dry between waterings. Ensure sharp drainage.

Uses: perhaps the most showy flowering plants, ideal for window boxes and hanging baskets.

Propagation: tubers are easiest. Plant them concave side up in a box of moist peat in spring in a temperature of about 16°C (61°F). Remove female flowers (with seed capsule) to get bigger male flowers. Begonia seed is very fine, so sow thinly and do not cover, in early spring at 16-19°C (61-65°F). Take stem cuttings for tuberous kinds, leaf or stem for fibrous kinds.

The vividness of colour, the quantity of bloom and wide range of types have made Begonias a popular variety.

Beloperone

SHRIMP PLANT

(*Beloperone guttata*)
Family Acanthaceae, a genus of about 30 evergreen shrubs native to parts of tropical America.

Habit: small, woody-stemmed, bearing soft green leaves and brownish-rose bracts beneath which grow the little tubular blooms.

Description: this little plant is mainly of interest for the little shrimp-like bracts, which should have as much colour as possible. Pinch out growing tips to induce bushy growth.

Needs: the soil must never be allowed to dry out yet must not be too wet, and the plant needs regular feeding. It likes a light but not sunny position and a temperature of about 18°C (64°F), winter and summer.

Dangers: cold; hot sun; dry roots; wet roots; inadequate feeding; poor light.

Uses: a good window plant, preferably facing west for good but not strong light.

Propagation: by cuttings inserted in peat in a propagating case at about 20°C (68°F).

Billbergia

Bougainvillea

ANGEL'S TEARS

(*Billbergia nutans*)
Family Bromeliaceae, a genus of some 50 stemless herbaceous plants from South America.
Habit: about 10-15 grey-green, slender leaves some 30 cm (12 in) long and a long pink scape bearing pink and green blooms.
Description: the attractive flowers are short-lived but the pink bracts stay on as with other bromeliads. It grows quickly and forms clusters of plants which should be separated.
Needs: these are easy plants to grow and make no special demands for light or warmth.
Dangers: over-wet soil; overcrowding.
Uses: as a temporary house plant when in flower. A group planted in a hanging basket will stay decorative for about a month.
Propagation: knock the plants from their pot and separate them gently. After potting, keep the soil almost dry for the first few weeks to encourage the growth of new roots.

BOUGAINVILLEA

(*Bougainvillea glabra*)
Family Nyctaginaceae, a genus of seven or eight species of shrubs, trees and climbers from tropical South America.
Habit: a strong climber with bright-green small leaves and papery flower-like bracts.
Description: Bougainvillea is a difficult plant to grow in the home, for it needs very good light. It is deciduous, so that in winter the bare stems have no interest nor attraction. In spring the bracts begin to colour and by the summer the climber exhibits a mass of splendid purple, mauve, pink, white or yellow inflorescences in their typical groups of three. The tiny flowers in their centres are insignificant against the vivid and papery bracts.
Needs: plenty of good light, even sunlight for periods. Temperatures need not be high, in the neighbourhood of 10-15°C (50-60°F) and even a little lower in winter, when the plant is kept almost dry. Support must be provided for the long climbing trails.
Dangers: lack of light; too hot and dry a situation; lack of fresh air.
Uses: ideal for a conservatory or even a garden room which has plenty of light and can be ventilated to give fresh air.

Propagation: after winter dormancy the plant should be pruned to shape and size. Pruned pieces can be grown as cuttings in sand and peat with bottom heat.

SLIPPER FLOWER

(*Calceolaria herbeohybrida*)
Family Scrophulariaceae, a genus of about 200 species of herbs or shrubs mainly from South America.
Habit: the herbaceous Calceolaria is distinguished by the characteristic brightly-coloured pouched flowers.
Description: small, compact plants with slightly crinkled green leaves and many spotted pouched flowers in yellow, orange and red.
Needs: a light situation out of direct sun. They should be kept cool rather than over-warm with the soil kept moist at all times. Regular light feeding keeps plants growing.
Dangers: hot and dry conditions. Strongly growing plants may attract summer greenfly.
Uses: a vivid, bright and cheerful plant for the summer living room which is kept cool and airy or for the ventilated garden room.
Propagation: sow seeds, which are very small and fine, in mid-summer in pots or boxes and just cover lightly with sand. Pot on in autumn to flower the following year.

Calceolaria hybrids can be large- or small-flowered, summer or winter blooming. All are brightly coloured.

ITALIAN BELLFLOWER

(*Campanula isophylla*)
Family Campanulaceae, a genus of some 250 species of mainly perennial herbs.
Habit: a prostrate perennial plant with toothed oval leaves and many star-like flowers, lilac blue with grey centres.
Description: the trailing *C. isophylla* is popular as a rock plant as well as being grown indoors. There is a white variety, *C. i. alba,* which is popular as a pot plant, as is the mauve variety *C. i. mayii.*
Needs: a cool, light, airy situation in the home. Plants must be kept moist at all times and fed regularly when in flower.
Dangers: hot sun and dryness at the roots. Plants will quickly droop under these conditions and are unlikely to recover.
Uses: because of its trailing habit, Campanula is particularly suited to a hanging basket.
Propagation: take cuttings in a peaty-sand mixture in spring or early summer. Pinch out growing tips at an early stage to encourage bushy growth.

Campanula

CHRYSANTHEMUM

House plant Chrysanthemums are a fairly recent product of scientific and semi-mechanized flower growing. Pots are produced all the year round bearing identical plants with identical blooms and they are wonderful value for money. Careful research has proved that plants of a certain height and a certain size are most popular, so they are produced to meet this demand. At certain times of the year, perhaps for holidays or festivals, demand increases so production can also be increased to meet this demand. There are occasions when the demand for potted Chrysanthemums is lower than the call for cut flowers for florist work, so it is also possible to grow stems of Chrysanthemums to standard lengths most suitable for their needs. By these means, the potted Chrysanthemum has become an inexpensive, almost uniform product available all over the world.

(*Chrysanthemum* hybrids)
Family Compositae, a genus of more than 100 annual and perennial herbs and sub-shrubs from most parts of the world except Australia and New Zealand.
Habit: Chrysanthemums grown as house plants are small, lavishly flowered and available regardless of natural season.
Description: pots usually have five or six plants in them and the flowers are usually Decorative or Pompon, of uniform size and a height of about 40 cm (15 in).
Needs: a light and airy situation in a cool room. Roots should be kept just moist at all times, regardless of the season.

The Chrysanthemum is said to be the most popular of all flowers among gardeners. Indoors, the beautiful blooms may last for several weeks.

There are many colours and types of Chrysanthemum available. Examples of flower heads are Intermediate (right) where the florets are loosely arranged, and Pompon, where florets are more tightly grouped.

Dangers: hot, dry atmosphere and full sun.
Uses: a splendid home decoration and gift plant which looks fresh and attractive for almost its entire life. Plants last considerably longer than cut flowers.
Propagation: when flowers have faded pots can be planted in the garden, where they will revert to natural height and season.

CINERARIA

(*Cineraria cruenta*)
Family Compositae, a genus of about 25 species of shrubs, sub-shrubs and herbs, mainly from South Africa.
Habit: a free-flowering perennial herb best grown as an annual. House plants are hybrids.
Description: there are many different types of Cineraria, all bearing daisy-like flowers of almost every colour. There are the tall Stellata types, double types, dwarf Multiflora and large-flowered, all highly colourful and easy to grow from seed. The Nana Multiflora strain, producing dozens of brilliantly coloured small flowers growing above the neat, small leaves, is perhaps the best for the home grower. Stellata types — taller, 'starrier', and with a wide range of brilliant colours — are also popular.
Needs: Cinerarias need plenty of light, but will quickly wilt in strong, direct sun. They prefer cool conditions with a certain amount of ventilation, but keep out of draughts.
Dangers: hot, dry conditions; attack from greenfly and blackfly.
Uses: the cheerful and vivid flowers create colour and interest in a room. They are also splendid plants for public places and exhibitions.
Propagation: seeds are easily obtained and easy to sow. By sowing a succession in the late spring it is possible to have flowers throughout the winter. Sow thinly and, when the seedlings are large enough to handle, transfer them to their individual small pots. They can be potted on to 13 cm (5 in) pots after a few weeks and will grow well in these if they are fed and watered regularly.

Cineraria

CALAMONDIN ORANGE

(*Citrus mitis*)
Family Rutaceae, a genus of about 10-15 species of evergreen fruiting trees or shrubs.
Habit: dwarf, spineless orange tree which bears blossom and fruit while still small.
Description: unlike commercial citrus trees, which grow to 2 m (6 ft) or more and take several years before they bear a crop, the *C. mitis* is normally on sale when only about 60 cm (2 ft) tall. At this stage it already bears miniature oranges and possibly a simultaneous crop of sweetly-scented flowers.
Needs: the Calamondin Orange is one of the very few house plants which needs so much light that it can stand in a south-facing window even in summer, or placed out on a sun-baked terrace. This means that the soil will dry out quickly, so the plants must receive frequent watering. However, a wet root system can also be fatal to the plant so it is necessary to have an efficient and sharply-drained soil mixture.
Dangers: lack of sufficient light; wet or dry roots. Plants can be top heavy so should be grown in clay pots, not plastic.
Uses: a very attractive and decorative tree. The blossoms are dainty, white and very sweetly-scented.
Propagation: this is a task for the expert. Fruiting is assisted by hand-pollinating the flowers with a soft brush.

GOLDFISH PLANT

(*Columnea banksii*)
Family Gesneriaceae. A genus of about 100 evergreen herbs or sub-shrubs, climbers and trailers.
Habit: trailing or creeping shrub with small, tough, dark-green leaves and

Citrus

The sweetly scented blooms of Citrus mitis *will produce fruit more certainly if sprayed occasionally and hand-pollinated with a small brush.*

The trails of a well grown Columnea will hang for 1-2 m (3-6 ft), making a curtain of foliage studded with brilliant blooms. If grown in a hanging basket always ensure that the roots are kept moist.

vivid orange-red flowers produced in early spring.
Description: this is a plant which should be grown in a hanging basket so that the long trails of dark-green, glossy leaves and the many bright 'parrot bill' flowers can be seen to the best advantage in the late winter or early spring.
Needs: Columneas should be kept fairly warm at about 20°C (68°F) and always moist at the roots. They require a little light but not direct sun. In midwinter it is worth dropping its temperature to about 10°C (50°F) and keeping plants almost dry for a few weeks to encourage the growth of more flower buds on the trails.
Dangers: plants placed high in a room often suffer from draughts of rising heat.
Uses: a spectacular plant for a garden or living room when in full flower and leaf.
Propagation: cuttings about 10 cm (4 in) long should be inserted in a warm propagating case where they will quickly root. Pot on twice to get strong, mature plants with long trails ready for flowering.

CYCLAMEN
(*Cyclamen persicum*)
Family Primulaceae. A genus of about 15 species of herbs grown from corms from the Mediterranean area.
Habit: the pot or florist's Cyclamen is a form of *C. persicum* which varies widely.
Description: the large flowers are white, pink, red or streaked rising above almost heart-shaped leaves, sometimes brilliantly marked with a silver band. They grow from a corm at the surface of the soil. The beautiful flowers can be very long-lasting with a constant succession for many months.
Needs: for a long and decorative life the Cyclamen must be kept out of hot and stuffy rooms and placed in an atmosphere both cool, 10-13°C (50-55°F), and well-ventilated. The roots must be kept moist at all times, but never too wet. Light should be good, although the plant should never be allowed to stay in direct sun.
Dangers: hot, airless rooms and dry soil will quickly kill a Cyclamen.
Uses: a superb gift plant.
Propagation: after flowering, as the plant fades, reduce the water until dry, then store until new growth begins in midsummer. Remove and repot in good fresh soil, the corm only half buried.

Cyclamen

CAPE HEATH

(*Erica hyemalis*)
Family Ericaceae. A genus of more than 500 species of evergreen shrubs, mostly from South Africa.

Habit: winter flowering heather, white or pink, with an upright habit of growth.

Description: daintier, with larger bells and more flowers than outdoor heathers. Plants are usually sold in full flower. They cannot take warm, dry conditions and soon shed their leaves and then their flowers. They should be given a situation in the home where the temperature never rises above about 10°C (50°F) and where there is plenty of cool humidity.

Needs: a cool, light, airy situation and moisture at the roots. Always water and spray with rain water.

Dangers: nothing kills indoor heathers so quickly as a hot, dry, stuffy atmosphere such as is frequently found in the home in winter.

Uses: a pretty little gift pot, or as a temporary decoration.

Propagation: in the spring it is possible to root short cuttings in a propagating case at a temperature of about 20°C (68°F).

The little white or pink bells of Erica hyemalis, E. gracilis *and* E. nivalis *need cool, moist conditions.*

Fuchsia

FUCHSIA

(*Fuchsia* hybrids)
Family Oenotheraceae. A genus of 100 species of shrubs and small trees from South America and New Zealand.

Habit: a wide range of flowering and fruiting shrubs, most tender, some hardy, up to 2.5-3.5 m (8-10 ft) in height. The small, light-green leaves are faintly toothed. Pendant, bell-like flowers are usually red and white, red and purple or pink.

Description: the shape, size and colours of the flowers differ widely and it is possible to grow a collection which will give a constant succession of bloom. It is best to grow them outdoors or in the greenhouse and to bring them indoors for a brief spell as they come into flower.

Needs: like most basically outdoor plants they need cool surroundings and constant moisture at their roots.

Dangers: dry air; dry roots; a hot situation.

Uses: as a temporary plant indoors while at their most beautiful, then outdoors.

Propagation: by easily-rooted cuttings.

GLOXINIA

(*Sinningia speciosa*)
Family Gesneriaceae. A genus of about 20 species of low-growing herbs, mainly from Brazil.
Habit: small, low-growing, with large, slightly crinkled leaves and large, velvety, deeply-coloured bell flowers.
Description: flowers are scarlet, pink, crimson, purple, mauve, violet and white and many variations and combinations of these. Plants will develop tubers which can be retained and grown on from year to year.
Needs: some warmth and a light, humid situation. Give plenty of water at the roots when growing but the soil must never be too wet. Feed regularly when flowering.
Dangers: cold; draughts; dry soil; sun; water on foliage or on the open blooms.
Uses: a brilliant plant to grow indoors in humid, well-lit conditions.
Propagation: can be grown from seed quite easily and later tubers can be kept from year to year and repotted after a period of rest and drought. Cuttings root well.

WAX FLOWER

(*Hoya carnosa*)
Family Asclepiadaceae. A genus of about 70 species of climbing or decumbent evergreen shrubs.

The velvety, bell-like flowers of Gloxinias come in many colours. Sometimes difficult in the home, they need warmth and humidity.

Habit: a climber with pointed oval leaves and pinkish-white, star-shaped waxen flowers.
Description: given a warm, light situation and a large enough pot a Hoya will soon climb to the ceiling, but if the beautiful flowers are the attraction it is better to keep the plant in a small pot. On the other hand there are variegated forms which produce fewer flowers but wonderful cream and green leaves. The flowers, which hang in little pendant clusters, are incredibly delicate, looking as though carved out of wax, making a beautiful pinky-creamy ball.
Needs: Hoyas need good light and are best grown in a window. They should be kept moderately warm and the pot must be kept well moistened at all times. Feed lightly but regularly when growing.
Dangers: cold; lack of light.
Uses: as an attractive window climber. Flowers are popular for delicate bouquets.
Propagation: pieces of woody stem inserted in a peat-sand mixture will root quickly.

HYDRANGEA

(*Hydrangea* varieties)
Family Saxifragaceae. A genus of about 35 species of shrubs.
Habit: a deciduous shrub with large, soft, toothed green leaves and flowers in a compact dome — pink, red, white, blue, purple.
Description: pot-grown Hydrangeas have been bred to produce large heads of vivid and compact colour. Some are artificially treated with chemicals in the soil to produce blue flowers, and an acid soil is necessary for this colour. In alkaline or neutral soils blooms are always pink. White remains white regardless of soil. Hydrangeas can go out into the garden after they have been enjoyed indoors, growing well either in the soil or in a large pot, filled with a rich, loamy soil mixture holding moisture.
Needs: the predominant need of the Hydrangea is water. In warm weather it may need watering more than once a day and the root ball must never be allowed to become dry. Light must be good to get brightly coloured flowers and the situation should be cool. After flowering, the heads should be removed, and in winter plants should be kept almost dry and fairly cool until growth begins again in about February or March.
Dangers: lack of water.
Uses: plants can sometimes be too large for the home after one or two years' growth. They are excellent for public buildings and for exhibitions.
Propagation: take cuttings from blind shoots in spring and insert singly in pots in a warm frame. Grow throughout summer and harden off outside in autumn.

Hydrangea

Hydrangeas can grow into large plants outdoors but in a pot they are more manageable. They must never be allowed to become too dry.

Hypocyrta

CLOG PLANT
(*Hypocyrta glabra*)
Family Gesneriaceae. A genus of about 12 species of small shrubs originating mainly from Brazil.
Habit: many small, fleshy, shining, dark-green leaves on erect stems and with many small, bulbous, orange-red flowers between.
Description: a plant bearing masses of little orange flowers that have given it the name of Goldfish Plant. The flowers last throughout the spring and summer as long as plants are kept fairly cool, in a light situation and the roots are kept moist. The plant never grows very large, so it can stay in a small pot.
Needs: good light. It will even take the sun for quite long periods but the roots must be kept moist at all times and temperatures should be kept low, with some humidity.
Dangers: too warm a situation; too dry an atmosphere; too dry a root ball.
Uses: this is a pretty little plant, neat, clean and not given to dropping leaves or flowers. It trails attractively.
Propagation: cuttings from a Hypocyrta root quite easily if inserted in a warm, humid propagating case.

BUSY LIZZIE
(*Impatiens* hybrids)
Family Balsaminacae. A genus of about 500 species of annual or biennial herbs.
Habit: a small, fleshy plant with flowers of many colours and soft leaves, either light-green or so dark as to be almost black.
Description: because of their popularity much hybridization has taken place and there are now many different varieties, mainly derived from *I. holstii* and *I. petersiana*. Flowers are now larger and more vivid and plants are becoming tougher and losing some of their soft and sappy type of growth. Flowers are red, pink, orange, magenta, white and some are bi-coloured.
Needs: good light is essential, but Busy Lizzies cannot stand direct sunlight for more than a few minutes, because their soft and sappy growth transpires moisture more quickly than it can be drawn up.
Dangers: dryness at the roots; hot sun; lack of light; attack by greenfly.
Uses: a colourful, easy plant.
Propagation: plants grow easily from seed or from cuttings.

One of the reasons for the popularity of the Busy Lizzie is its hardiness. It will flourish with a little watering and feeding, with good light and a little warmth.

JASMINE

(*Jasminum polyanthum*)
Family Oleaceae. A genus of 200 climbers, trailers and erect shrubs from many parts.
Habit: a strongly-growing climber with glossy dark-green leaves and highly perfumed flowers appearing in late winter.
Description: the starry, white flowers are the main attraction. The trails grow quickly if they like their situation and it is necessary to give them some support to keep them within bounds. They can be cut back once they have finished flowering.
Needs: cool and airy conditions with as strong light as possible without direct sunlight. Soil must be kept moist at all times and regular feeding will keep the trails and the fragrant flowers growing. Spray daily to provide humidity for the foliage.
Dangers: a hot and dry atmosphere; too rampant growth without control.
Uses: this plant is better for a conservatory than a living room.
Propagation: cuttings will root quite easily in a warm, humid propagating case.

Jasminum

GERANIUM

(*Pelargonium* varieties)
Family Geraniaceae. A genus of about 250 species of herbs, erect or trailing, some shrubby.
Habit: widely varied family divided into distinct groups and consisting today almost entirely of cultivated hybrids.
Description: Regal or Show Pelargoniums are large-flowered with large green leaves. In the home they will flower for nine months of the year if the best varieties are selected. Colours are white, pink, red and a dark mauve, but most flowers have two or perhaps three colours in them. Zonal Pelargoniums all have decorated leaves, usually with a horseshoe of darker colour. With the Zonals come the Fancy-leaved, which can vary from being a formal bi-colour to having four or five colours. Flowers vary widely in colour and size. The Ivy-Leaved Pelargoniums have trailing stems and foliage shaped like an ivy leaf, but usually variegated with cream and green. They are particularly good for hanging baskets. Scented-leaved Pelargoniums are not so vividly flowered but have a strong perfume when the leaves are pinched or brushed.
Needs: all Geraniums need good light and some will enjoy direct sun

Pelargoniu

for periods. They do not like to be too warm, enjoying a cool and airy situation, so long as it is frost-free. They need to rest for a period in winter and to be repotted later. High potash fertilizers will increase leaf colour, as will lightly shaded conditions.
Uses: probably the world's most popular flowering plants. Geraniums are widely grown indoors and in the garden because of their vivid flowers and attractive foliage.
Propagation: Geraniums grow easily from cuttings.

Primula acaulis
Primula malacoides

The versatile Geranium provides a show of colour right through the summer and grows anywhere.

PRIMULA

(*Primula* species)
Family Primulaceae. A genus of more than 500 species of mainly small alpine perennial herbs.
Habit: usually small plants growing on a rhizomatous rootstock with many variations.
Description: the three main varieties are *P. sinensis,* with fairly large flowers in several colours, *P. malacoides,* with small and dainty flowers, and *P. obconica,* a stronger plant with larger flowers.
Needs: all the Primulas prefer cool to warm conditions, moist roots at all times and an airy atmosphere. Some will flower for almost 12 months a year if fed regularly and if dead flower heads are promptly removed.
Dangers: a hot and dry situation.
Uses: a good indoor decorative pot plant.
Propagation: sow seed in early spring, very finely and thinly because they are small, and place in a propagator at about 16°C (60°F). Transfer seedlings to pots when they can be handled. Feed regularly.

AFRICAN VIOLET

(*Saintpaulia ionantha*)
Family Gesnariaceae. A genus of about six species of perennial herbs from Africa.
Habit: small, low-growing, frequently with hairy leaves on short stems and with flowers of white, pink, red, blue, purple or bi-coloured, single and double.
Description: although there are probably thousands of varieties, all come from *S. ionantha.* Their virtues are the dainty flowers and the way they can sometimes be kept in bloom for an entire year. The almost round leaves are hairy or smooth, light- or dark-green and sometimes have a purple underside.
Needs: Saintpaulias need some warmth and humidity but must not be sprayed nor have water on their flowers or leaves. They must have good light and will even accept sun for brief periods so long as their roots are moist. They should be allowed almost to dry out between waterings and should be fed occasionally with a dilute fertilizer.
Dangers: cold; lack of light; wet roots. They dislike draughts and are sensitive to impurities in the air such as gases, smoke and dust.
Uses: Saintpaulias will grow anywhere in the house.
Propagation: leaf cuttings will grow easily in water or a peat-sand mixture.

Saintpaulia varieties include pink and white flowers. African Violets can be easy to grow, flowering the year through, but they need clean air to do really well.

WINTER CHERRY

(*Solanum capsicastrum*)
Family Solanaceae. A genus of more than 900 species, mainly herbs, from most areas.
Habit: small shrub with dark-green leaves and many round, orange or yellow berries.
Description: a difficult plant to keep in the home for long periods because it must have good light. It drops its leaves and berries in a hot, polluted atmosphere. When in flower, plants must be sprayed daily to assist pollination and ensure a heavy crop of berries. The berries are the most decorative part of the plant, but they are slightly poisonous and should be kept away from children.
Needs: good light, some warmth and humidity.
Dangers: poor light; hot, dry air.
Uses: a pleasant and interesting plant for a bare but bright window sill.
Propagation: take cuttings in spring or sow seed from ripe berries.

WHITE SAILS

(*Spathiphyllum wallisii*)
Family Araceae. A genus of about 30 species of evergreen perennial herbs from South America.

Habit: bright-green, spear-shaped leaves and a longer peduncle bearing a white spathe with a central erect spadix.

Description: the clumps of leaves spring from the soil surface on a short stalk and surround the curious flowers that stand above them. The flowers are tiny and stud the white spadix which grows in the centre of the larger, white spathe.

Needs: warm conditions where the roots are always moist. Although a temperature of about 18-21°C (64-70°F) should be aimed at, no harm will come to the plants if it drops a little lower than this on some occasions.

Dangers: dryness at the roots will quickly kill the plant as will hot, dry air and the direct rays of summer sun.

Uses: particularly useful in the home because it is one of the few flowering plants that will tolerate a fairly shaded situation.

Propagation: by division of root clumps, prised apart, planted in a peaty soil.

The Winter Cherry is not a cherry at all and the berries should never be eaten. They make the little plant look bright and attractive in winter.

Spathiphyllum

The dainty trumpet flowers of the Cape Primrose come in many colours.

CAPE PRIMROSE
(*Streptocarpus* hybrids)
Family Gesneriaceae. A genus of about 80 species of herbs mainly from South Africa.
Habit: large, coarse, wrinkled, low-growing leaves below flower stems producing many trumpet blooms, red, pink, blue and white.
Description: newer varieties of Streptocarpus have better colours and are longer lasting. They now flower right through spring and summer and with luck and care it is possible to have plants in flower almost right through the year.
Needs: plants must have good light but must be protected against strong sunlight for long periods. The roots should be kept moist at all times but a little less water can be given in the winter months.
Dangers: dry soil; hot sun; hot stuffy atmosphere in the house.
Uses: colourful and decorative plants, especially in a group arrangement.
Propagation: mainly by seed, which can be sown in succession from late winter to midsummer so that young plants will always be coming along. Or leaves can be removed and their stems inserted in a peat-sand mixture at about 18°C (64°F).

BLUE-FLOWERED TORCH
(*Tillandsia cyanea*)
Family Bromeliaceae. A genus of about 400 species of stemless herbaceous plants, most epiphytic.
Habit: greenish-brown, slim, strap-like leaves form a central clump from which rises a flat, even series of bracts.
Description: the Tillandsia is of little interest until the inflorescence begins to grow and change from a dull grey-green to a beautiful clear pink, producing tiny blue flowers. Although the blooms themselves are short-lived, the bracts stay attractive and interesting for months.
Needs: a highly tolerant plant that will live with little attention.
Dangers: frost; wetness at the roots for long periods.
Uses: a striking, decorative plant.
Propagation: Tillandsia will fill its pot in time, and although the resulting proliferation of pink bracts may look attractive, it is better to divide them.

Vriesia

FLAMING SWORD

(*Vriesia splendens*)
Family Bromeliaceae. A genus of more than 100 species of perennial herbaceous plants.

Habit: a typical bromeliad, with strap-like leaves rising from a central vase, green banded horizontally with brown and a tall scape bearing a bright-red sword-like inflorescence, from which emerge the many tubular yellow flowers.

Description: the grey-green leaves, horizontally banded with chocolate brown, arch out from the central cup. From the centre grows the flower scape, growing tall above the leaves and producing a waxen sword or spear of vivid red. After a time there appear between the close and overlapping bracts a series of yellow flowers, short-lived compared with the lasting bracts.

Needs: an easy plant to grow. Keep the central vase filled with water. Make sure the plant has moderately good light and a reasonably warm temperature.

Dangers: wet soil, which will result in root rot; frost.

Uses: it is the 'flaming sword' that is the most striking feature of this plant and which will provide colour and interest.

Propagation: all the vase or rosette

The banded colours of Vriesia leaves are always striking even without the splendid inflorescence.

bromeliads produce offsets which grow from the soil beside the parent plant and which can be cut with roots and potted.

Tillandsia

CACTI AND SUCCULENTS

Cacti have no leaves but have instead swollen and succulent stems which serve as water reservoirs. Succulents are usually thick and fleshy also, but most have leaves of some form. Both groups store water in their bodies and can withstand long periods of direct sun.

Agave

The small, thick, spatulate leaves of Aeonium tabuliforme *are spaced and interleaved with mathematical precision, almost like the scales of a fish in the young plants.*

SAUCER PLANT

(*Aeonium tabuliforme*)
Family Crassulaceae. A genus of about 40 species of mainly low-growing, rosette-forming succulents.
Habit: a succulent with light-green leaves precisely arranged in rosettes.
Description: flower spikes rise from the stems bearing many pale yellow blooms, strong and long-lasting. The chunky, flat and sessile leaves open out as the flower spikes begin to grow. The plant dies after it has flowered.
Needs: plenty of good light but not too much heat. Water lavishly in summer and keep almost dry in winter.
Dangers: wet roots in winter will kill the plant, as will dry roots in summer.
Uses: an attractive plant both when immature and when coming into flower.
Propagation: remove one or two medium-sized leaves and allow to dry for a day before placing in a sandy compost.

CENTURY PLANT

(*Agave americana*)
Family Agavaceae. A genus of about 300 species of succulent perennials.
Habit: rosette-forming, low-growing plant with tall, central flower spike.
Description: *A. americana* can grow

Aloe

too large for the home unless confined to a small pot. It is slow-growing and gains its popular name from the saying that it flowers only once in 100 years. Smaller than *A. americana* are *A. filifera, A. parviflora, A. stricta* and *A. victoriae-reginae*.
Needs: fresh air. Place plants outside in summer and keep them cool in winter.
Dangers: wet roots are to be avoided with all succulents. Mealy bugs sometimes collect in inaccessible places in leaf joints and on the roots.
Uses: large plants suit a protected patio, but smaller ones can stay indoors safely.
Propagation: all these Agaves except *A. victoriae-reginae* produce offsets.

PARTRIDGE-BREASTED ALOE

(*Aloe variegata*)
Family Liliaceae. A genus of about 300 species of rosette-forming perennials.
Habit: a series of chunky, spear-shaped leaves overlapping and emanating from one point. They are variegated dark- and light-green.
Description: the leaves are attractively marked, paler beneath and darker at the tips. These leaves can reach a height of 30 cm (12 in) but are usually smaller and surrounded by a number of tiny offsets in the soil around the central stemless base of the plant. The leaves are in three ranks and have tiny white, saw-toothed edges to them. This is a succulent which prefers to be out of the sun and should not be too heavily watered. In spring a flower stem appears which will grow to 30 cm (12 in) and produce at the top a series of tubular orange flowers.
Needs: *A. variegata* will grow well indoors in a light spot. Place outdoors in shade in summer and in winter keep almost dry in a temperature no lower than 5°C (41°F).

A. flagelliformis has shining green stems, later turning greyish.

Dangers: wet roots in winter. Mealy bug may attack both leaves and roots. Clear this with a watercolour paint brush dipped in methylated spirits.
Uses: in flower or immature, this makes an attractive display plant.
Propagation: remove offsets and allow to dry for two days before potting.

RAT'S TAIL CACTUS

(*Aporocactus flagelliformis*)
Family Cactaceae. A genus of about six species of flowering cacti.
Habit: low-growing, much-branched, with slender stems, quick-growing, free-flowering.
Description: stems are about 1 cm ($\frac{1}{2}$ in) thick and can grow to 1 m (3 ft) long, green and covered with brown spines. Often grafted onto a taller cactus to lift the 'tails' from the soil.
Needs: a rich soil with some leaf mould. Give plenty of water in summer, less in winter, with a minimum temperature of about 5°C (41°F).
Dangers: wet roots; mealy bug; red spider in too dry an atmosphere.
Uses: an interesting cactus which produces pretty tubular magenta flowers.
Propagation: by seed or by removing a stem, allowing to dry and then potting in a firm, rich, but well-drained soil.

MOTHER OF THOUSANDS

(*Bryophyllum daigremontianum*)
Family Crassulaceae. A genus of about 20 species of fleshy, succulent sub-shrubs, glaucous green.
Habit: the leaves, up to 15 cm (3 in) long, heavily-toothed, bear many tiny plantlets between their indentations.
Description: the tiny plantlets can be placed on the soil surface where they will grow, or they will fall by themselves to the soil in the pot and begin to grow there. The attractive glaucous green leaves, arrow shaped, have reddish-purple irregular markings. The pendant, yellowish-pink flowers usually appear in winter if the plant is kept warm and well fed.
Needs: plenty of water, warmth and good light in summer. Direct sun will do no harm as long as the roots are kept moist. Reduce watering in winter and keep in maximum light.
Dangers: lack of water in summer and too much in winter; low temperatures.
Uses: an interesting display plant.
Propagation: best and easiest by means of the tiny plantlets. Place these on a damp sand or peat surface, where the little root hairs will quickly grow.

Bryophyllum

OLD MAN CACTUS

(*Cephalocereus senilis*)
Family Cactaceae.
Habit: a columnar cactus with close areoles and weak grey bristles like coarse hairs, silkier when immature.
Description: a popular cactus because of the long white hairs that cover the entire plant. If these become dusty or matted, they can be washed in a mild soapy solution and then combed out and left to dry in the sun. A very slow-growing specimen of *C. senilis* will grow to 12 m (40 ft) in its native Mexico.
Needs: full sunshine, plenty of water in summer, almost none in deep winter.
Dangers: *C. senilis* does not have a woody trunk, so can be attacked by root rot.
Uses: an interesting cactus which grows so slowly that it can be kept for many years.
Propagation: from seed or from cuttings taken from the stem and allowed to dry.

Tough and slow-growing, the white 'hair' of Cephalocereus senilis *can be 'washed and set'.*

COLUMN CACTUS

(*Cereus peruvianus*)
Family Cactaceae. A genus of more than 200 species of succulent trees, shrubs and climbers.
Habit: a terrestrial cactus with a cylindrical stem of some 5-8 ribs.
Description: a difficult cactus to name or identify correctly, partly because of cross-hybridization and partly because it has a different form when young. The mature 5-8 ribs (some say 6-9) are thick, obtuse and slightly notched. It will not flower until up to 1 m (3 ft) tall.
Needs: plenty of water during summer months. Keep almost dry in the winter resting period. Place in direct sun.
Dangers: wet roots in winter and too dry roots in the hotter days of summer.
Uses: although this cactus will not flower while small and immature, it is a useful, decorative plant.
Propagation: by seed, or by cuttings at any time of year but preferably during summer. A stem top allowed to dry for a few days will root quickly in sand or a peat-sand soil.

The curious twining habit of Ceropegia woodii *shows off the chunky grey-purple leaves and flowers.*

HEARTS ENTWINED

(*Ceropegia woodii*)
Family Asclepiadaceae. A genus of a small number of species of mainly climbing plants, with or without leaves, with tuberous roots and unusual flowers.
Habit: few leaves on trailing wiry stems which carry occasional tubular purple-grey enclosed flowers.
Description: an unusual succulent with fleshy, heart-shaped purple-grey leaves at intervals along the trailing wiry stems together with occasional little tubers which can be removed to form new plants.
Needs: plenty of water when growing well, little in winter. Some warmth.
Dangers: few leaves mean little transpiration, so watch watering carefully.
Uses: an engaging plant which can be trained around a hooped wire support to show off the curious foliage and flowers.
Propagation: by using the little tubers carried on the stems as cuttings.

Cereus

Cleistocactus straussii *is another of the group of cacti which almost hide their spines and areoles with many hair-like bristles.*

Crassula argentea

SILVER TORCH CACTUS

(*Cleistocactus straussii*)
Family Cactaceae. A genus of six species of cacti with erect stems and bright spines.
Habit: a tall-growing cactus with up to 25 ribs and inconspicuous spines hidden by the white hairs produced at the areoles.
Description: a popular species because of the hairy surface, parts of which are even soft enough to be handled with bare hands. It often grows to a considerable height, up to 1 m (3 ft) or so, in which case it should be staked unless growing securely.
Needs: all cacti need a resting period, usually winter, which should be spent almost dry. Water should be applied only when the plant is growing.
Dangers: cold; wet roots in winter.
Uses: a pleasant cactus to grow in a group.
Propagation: one or more of the clumps can be removed, dried and potted up.

CRASSULA SPECIES

Family Crassulaceae. A genus of some 200-300 species of evergreen succulents, mainly perennial.
Habit: very varied, from tiny types like twigs or stones to considerable shrubs too large to grow in the home.
Description: some of the most popular include the so-called Jade Plants, *C. arborescens, C. lactea, C. obliqua* and *C. portulaca,* all with fleshy green leaves. By contrast, *C. lycopodioides* is completely different, growing much-branched with slim upright stems composed of tiny flat green leaves in which the almost invisible flowers grow. *C. corallina* has short, thick leaves which are tightly packed around the stems.
Needs: in general all Crassulas can be treated like cacti. Give plenty of water in summer, good light and very little water in winter.
Dangers: like cacti, Crassulas dislike wet roots.
Uses: depending on the plants, most of the indoor Crassulas make first-class specimens for dish and bowl gardens, for they mix well.

Propagation: practically all can be increased by cuttings taken in summer in a well-drained peat-sand soil.

ECHEVERIA SPECIES

Family Crassulaceae. A genus of about 150 species of succulent plants with leaves always in the form of a tight rosette.
Habit: rosettes are often coloured, sometimes hairy, with bell-shaped flowers on stems.
Description: this section of the Crassula family also produces some beautiful and unusual plants for the home. *E. agavoides* is reminiscent of an agave — smaller, pale green; *E. bella* makes clumps and has orange-yellow flowers. Orange flowers also appear on *E. derenbergii*, rising just above the blue-grey leaf rosette. A much larger plant is *E. gibbiflora*, with leaves that will reach 25 cm (10 in) or so in length, grey-green, glaucous, and with the usual orange-red flowers. It has several varieties of interest. *E. harmsii* makes a dainty indoor plant with the attention on the orange and yellow bell-like flowers instead of the foliage. Some of the Echeverias have a soft, hairy, felted foliage, including *E. leucotricha* and *E. pulvinata* and *E. setosa*, all attractive and interesting.
Needs: plenty of water in summer, no water at all in winter unless the room is warm, then a little once a month only. The soil mixture must be open and well-drained.
Dangers: besides the normal risk of wet and cold soil, some of these Echeverias are sensitive to certain pesticides, notably malathion. The sensitive group are those with a glaucous appearance, an almost waxy surface with a bloom. The chemical can seriously damage this surface.
Uses: some of these plants will stand on their own but most look best in a group or in contrast with others.
Propagation: several means. Seed is easy. Cuttings can be taken, including leaves. Young shoots and flower scapes will root.

Echeveria harmsii

Echeveria agavoides

Echeveria gibbiflora metallica

Echeveria derenbergii

111

The Golden Barrel cactus, Echinocactus grusonii, *will grow to more than 1 m (3 ft) tall.*

GOLDEN BARREL CACTUS

(*Echinocactus grusonii*)
Family Cactaceae. A genus of about nine species of Hedgehog cacti.
Habit: light-green, globular cactus with yellow spines becoming white.
Description: *E. grusonii* will grow into a plant more than 1 m (3 ft) tall if given a large pot and plenty of time. It will only flower in the home if given really favourable conditions.
Needs: normal cactus treatment is necessary (see *Cleistocactus straussii*, page 110).
Dangers: normal precautions must be taken.
Uses: this rich golden-coloured cactus is very attractive and it is worth while trying to grow a large specimen so it can be seen to advantage.
Propagation: this cactus does not normally make offsets, so propagation must be from seed, just covered with soil and grown at a temperature of about 21°C (70°F).

EUPHORBIA SPECIES

Family Euphorbiaceae. A genus of some 2000 species of most kinds of plants except trees, including many succulents, most with a poisonous or irritating milky-white latex or sap.
Habit: succulent forms are several, some like cacti, some like shrubs.
Description: it is impossible to list all the succulent Euphorbias, but species include the following. *E. obesa* is almost spherical, a fat stem with eight wide ribs having only a shallow furrow between them. The colour is a grey-green, striped and banded with purple-brown lines and background washes. Tiny tubular flowers appear on the top of the sphere in summer. Older plants become columnar.

E. splendens or, more correctly, *E. milii*, has several forms. This is the plant popularly known as Crown of Thorns because of the particularly vicious spines and the tiny scarlet flowers like drops of blood. Strictly, *E. milii* is the small form with weak spines and succulent foliage; *E. m. splendens* is the larger and more generally seen form, which will grow to 2 m (6 ft) in height.

A third succulent Euphorbia is known as Stick Cactus, *E. tirucalii*, because of the stems which branch

Euphorbia splendens

Euphorbia tirucali

tree-like. This is also known as the Milk Bush, mainly because of the free flow of the milky white sap or latex that appears at any wound and which is poisonous to some. This same kind of latex may be found with other succulent forms, but less irritating. All these Euphorbias require normal care as for most cacti and succulents and are not particularly difficult to grow.

Euphorbia hermentiana

FLAMING KATY

(*Kalanchoe blossfeldiana*)
Family Crassulaceae. A genus of 200 species of tender shrubby perennials normally greenhouse-grown.

Habit: an erect bushy plant with chunky leaves and usually scarlet flowers in clusters on short leafless stems.

Description: this attractive flowering succulent is now produced in pink, white and yellow as well as the more familiar red. The normal flowering time is from early spring to early summer, but by using artificial light they can be made to flower conveniently early. Both plants and flowers are long lasting in the home with little special care.

Needs: good light; a little warmth in winter; plenty of water in summer with much less in winter.

Dangers: mainly low temperatures and a wet root system during winter cold. Attacks from mealy bug may be expected.

Uses: plants are sufficiently large to stand on their own as a bright splash of colour in winter, or with others in a group arrangement.

Propagation: seed can be sown in early spring or stem cuttings can be taken in summer, allowed to dry for a couple of days and then potted up in some warmth.

Kalanchoe blossfeldiana

Mammillaria bocasana

PINCUSHION CACTUS

(*Mammillaria bocasana*)
Family Cactaceae. A genus of more than 200 species of mainly greenhouse-grown perennials.
Habit: a small, blue-green cactus with white spines and soft, silky hairs.
Description: one of the easier and more popular of the cacti, mainly because it flowers easily if it receives the care it needs. *M. bocasana* will form cushion-like clumps in time, to make a plant 15 cm (6 in) across.
Needs: a well-drained, sandy soil so that, although watered well in summer, the roots stay only just moist. Water in plant crevices may set up an internal rotting process. Full sun is recommended, with plants quite dry during winter at temperatures no lower than about 5°C (41°F).
Dangers: cold, wet roots; water on plant.
Uses: a cactus that can stand on its own or in a group.
Propagation: seed can be sown in spring. Clumps can be removed and allowed to dry out for a day or two before being potted up.

GOLDFINGER CACTUS

(*Notocactus leninghausii*)
Family Cactaceae. A genus of 15 species of greenhouse perennials, mainly solitary and spherical.
Habit: cylindrical, light-green, up to 1 m (3 ft) in height, with about 30 ribs.
Description: this is a slow-growing species which may not flower unless enjoying the treatment it is receiving. The areoles have up to 15 golden

Golden Noctocactus leninghausii will produce lemon-yellow flowers with green outer petals during summer.

spines which give an appealing glow to the plant. If given too much water in summer this cactus sometimes bursts open, in which case it is best to slice off the undamaged portion and treat this as a separate cutting.
Needs: careful watering; exposure to hot sun in summer to prevent bursts.
Dangers: over-watering, winter and summer; too warm a situation in summer; attack by mealy bug.
Uses: ideal for a cactus tray with rocks and sand to simulate desert conditions.
Propagation: by seed, or by removing the top 15 cm (6 in) or so if grown too tall and treating this as a cutting.

OPUNTIA SPECIES

Family Cactaceae. A genus of 250 species, greenhouse perennials.
Habit: with cylindrical or globular jointed stems, often flattened into pads.

Description: the Opuntias or Prickly Pears are probably the best-known cacti. They came originally from the Americas but have colonized large parts of Europe and some are even classed as noxious weeds in Australia. The most frequently seen Opuntia is probably *O. microdasys* and its whiter form, *O. m. albispina,* known as Polka Dots. Another with equally flat pads but blue-grey and smooth is *O. robusta,* while one with spines of frightening dimensions is *O. leucotricha.* These Opuntias are a food plant in some places and their fruits can be bought in many parts of the world. *O. ficus-indica* is the original of the Prickly Pears and is said to produce the most edible fruits. Flowers are somewhat shy to appear unless plants are grown in bright sunlight.

Opuntias, particularly those with the flattened pads, are not as succulent as many cacti and so may require a little water during winter to retain their plump shapes or they may shrink and shrivel.

REBUTIA SPECIES

Rebutia miniscula

Family Cactaceae. A genus of about 50 species of tender, globular, much-hybridized, easily flowered and highly popular cacti.
Habit: globular, with small, close tubercles, many growing in clumps.
Description: popular and enjoyable cacti because they flower so easily. The flowers last about a week and open wide. Among the several species, one can mention *R. pygmaea,* with spirally arranged tubercles and $2\frac{1}{2}$ cm (1 in) wide rose-purple flowers. *R. miniscula* has been so hybridized as to be difficult to identify, but all with this name bear many flowers. The clump-forming *R. senilis* bears bright red flowers and *R. violaciflora* has much less frequently seen violet blooms on a spherical stem.

The Rebutias like to be on the dry side and flower best if given a period of considerable drought in winter, after which they flower freely. Generally, water should not be applied to any Rebutias until the red flower buds are seen around the bases of the plants. Because Rebutias flower easily they also seed easily, and so baby plants are often to be seen growing in the soil around the more mature parent plants above them.

The fact that it has been given popular names such as Bunny Ears Cactus and Polka Dot Cactus indicates that Opuntia microdasys *is a familiar and easily-managed plant.*

115

RHIPSALIDOPSIS ROSEA

(*Rhipsalidopsis rosea*)
Family Cactaceae. A genus of only two species of epiphytic cacti much hybridized with others.
Habit: stem segments are flat or triangular. Flowers can be red, white or pink.
Description: *R. rosea* may sometimes be a hybrid with *Schlumbergera gaertneri* or *Zygocactus truncatus* and sold under the name of Christmas Cactus. It is a dwarf, shrubby species, freely branching and with 5 cm (2 in) flowers.
Needs: moist warmth, with daily spraying during the hotter days of summer.
Dangers: mealy bug.
Uses: a wonderfully brilliant and effective plant when in full flower.
Propagation: joints can be broken off and allowed to dry for a day or two before being placed in a peat-sand mixture.

Flowers of Rhipsalidopsis rosea *have a complex beauty and make an attractive display.*

EASTER CACTUS

(*Schlumbergera gaertneri*)
Family Cactaceae. A genus of five species of perennial cacti.
Habit: free-flowering leaf succulents with flowers at the ends of the flat stems.

Schlumbergera gaertneri

Description: Easter cactus will grow to 1 m (3 ft) across and in spring will bear dozens of bright red flowers 6-7 cm ($2\frac{1}{2}$ in) across. These flowers and the new joints grow from the areoles on top of the stems.
Needs: Schlumbergeras need warmth, a rich soil, some humidity, plenty of light and a soil that is never allowed to dry out. They must have some protection from too bright a sun.
Dangers: more humidity is required than for most cacti and the soil must never be allowed to dry out or the buds will drop.
Uses: a good display plant, best hung high.
Propagation: take cuttings of joints in summer. Allow to dry then insert in soil.

SEDUM SIEBOLDII

(*Sedum sieboldii*)
Family Crassulaceae. A genus of 600 succulents, hardy and tender, evergreen and deciduous, annual and perennial. Suitable indoors and out.
Habit: a prostrate, half-hardy species with green, grey or yellow flat leaves
Description: a particularly attractive plant because of the delicacy of its leaf colour. The form usually seen and grown is *S. s. medio-variegatum* which dies down in winter. If confined

Sedum sieboldii *is an attractive spreading plant that will grow only 5-8 cm (2-3 in) tall but 30 cm (12 in) wde.*

Sedum pachyphyllum

to a cold greenhouse or an unheated room it will begin to grow again in the spring. The leaves are round and grey and flat clusters of pink flowers bloom in late summer. The species *S. pachyphyllum*, perhaps less frequently seen but still worth growing, has club-shaped leaves, blue-green with a red tip, and clusters of yellow flowers in late spring.

Needs: the soil should be more retentive of moisture than for that of other succulents. It should not be too rich or growth will be excessive at the cost of colour and flowers. Plants will gain from periods out of doors in summer. Temperatures should not drop below about 5°C (41°F) in winter.

Dangers: aphids and mealy bugs can be a danger in the growing season.

Uses: *Sedum sieboldii* is a useful plant because it can be grown indoors in a hanging basket, or in a patio pot or window box.

Propagation: both these species can be grown quite easily from cuttings, stem or leaf, allowed first to dry for a day.

CRAB CACTUS

(*Zygocactus truncatus*)
Family Cactaceae. A genus of five species of flowering perennial cacti.
Habit: freely-branching jointed stems, bright-green, with winter flowers in red, pink, white or purple.
Description: a popular group of winter flowering plants. Crab Cactus will grow to 30 cm (12 in) high and wide. The flat joints have 2-4 notches each side. Flowers appear in mid-winter.
Needs: rich, open soil; plenty of light and humidity; occasional feeds. A spell outdoors in summer ripens new growths.
Dangers: dry atmosphere; mealy bugs.
Uses: to provide colour during dark winter days.
Propagation: by joint cuttings in summer.

Zygocactus truncatus

BULBOUS PLANTS

Many plants grown in the home from bulbs, corms or tubers produce their flowers in winter. Some bulbs are specially prepared for early flowering, others appear at their normal period except that their growth is hastened by the artificial warmth of the home. Some bulbous flowers can be grown indoors year after year.

Clivia

KAFFIR LILY

(*Clivia miniata*)
Family Amaryllidaceae. A genus of three species of flowering bulbous plants.
Habit: large, evergreen leaves are sheathed at the base. Large, lily-like flowers come 12-20 to an umbel, yellow, through orange to red in vivid colour.
Description: the large, glossy, evergreen leaves are impressive and decorative. Flowers appear in early summer. All parts of this plant are large — crown, leaves and flower umbels — so the pot must be large enough to accommodate the plant when it has reached flowering size.
Needs: good, rich soil; plenty of water in spring and summer when growing well. In winter, bulbs should be allowed almost to dry out and can be kept quite cool. Keep out of direct sun. Wash leaves occasionally. Top dress with fresh soil annually in spring or repot if roots occupy too much space in the pot.
Dangers: too wet soil in winter.
Uses: a striking specimen when in flower.
Propagation: take offsets from mature plants when they are being repotted. Place these in good soil in a small pot and pot on each year until ready.

AUTUMN CROCUS

(*Colchicum byzantinum*)
Family Liliaceae. A genus of some 65 species of bulbous flowers like crocuses.
Habit: up to 20 flowers, usually lilac-rose, growing in a spathe from the bulb.
Description: very similar to the Meadow Saffron, *C. autumnale*, but with more and larger flowers.

Flowers will grow from the brown tunic of the bulb without even planting it, although of course it will grow better and last longer if the bulb

The lovely and large flowers of the Autumn Crocus will appear without soil, but will grow more lavishly if planted up in more orthodox fashion.

Crocus corms, packed into a pot, make a fresh and attractive display. This variety is Jeanne D'Arc.

CROCUS SPECIES

Family Iridaceae. A genus of more than 70 species of hardy flowering bulbous plants.

Habit: linear, dark-green leaves grow from small corms followed by the flower in the form of a slim corolla tube.

Description: crocuses to be grown in the home must first have a period in the garden or be kept in a cold part of the house. Wait until the flowers themselves are visible before bringing them indoors, otherwise they will not flower. Do not try to grow yellow varieties indoors, for they will not succeed, but grow instead the white, purple and mauve varieties.

Needs: a period of vernalization and the corms must then be almost in flower before being brought into the warmth.

Dangers: too warm a beginning; bringing corms indoors too early.

Uses: for decoration and colour in early spring.

Propagation: after flowering, plant the corms in garden soil, leaving the faded flowers and foliage still on them, to help to feed the corm. In subsequent years lift the corms when the leaves turn brown and remove and dry-off the offsets for a few days. Replant the largest, putting the smallest back.

is grown in bulb fibre or even water alone. The bulb is unusually large, 5 cm (2 in) or more long and wide. Colchicum flowers appear in autumn but the leaves do not grow until spring.

Needs: the soil or fibre should be kept just moist while the flowers are out, almost dry later.

Dangers: too much water or too little.

Uses: these large flowers are dramatic and deserve to be grown lavishly.

Propagation: bulbs should be planted in the garden after flowering and will produce offsets which can be separated.

119

This Hyacinth variety, Anne Marie, will look beautiful as well as filling the room with a sweet perfume.

AMARYLLIS

(*Hippeastrum* species)
Family Amaryllidaceae. A genus of 75 species of flowering bulbs.
Habit: large bulbs producing large, strap-like leaves and large vividly-coloured flowers, usually two or more per stem.
Description: perhaps the most dramatic of all the indoor flowering bulbs. It is possible to grow varieties in succession to provide blooms for the whole of the year. Bulbs should sit in tepid water for two or three days before planting in good, well-drained soil, leaving half the bulb out at the top. Place over a radiator or some other source of bottom heat until the buds have formed, then move to a warm, sunny situation.
Needs: some warmth; not too much water.
Dangers: low temperatures and badly drained soil will cause the bulb to rot.
Uses: the huge, dramatic and vivid blooms make this a strikingly beautiful plant to stand on its own.
Propagation: by seeds saved from the flowers, sown at about 16-18°C (61-64°F).

HYACINTH

(*Hyacinthus* species)
Family Liliaceae. A genus of 30 species of flowering bulbs.
Habit: strap-like, mid-green leaves and compact spikes of bell-shaped flowers.
Description: most Hyacinths except the Romans have a single spike per bulb. Their flowering season is fairly long and it is wise to find out the flowering time before buying. Hyacinths are among the most perfumed of all flowers, regardless of colour.
Needs: the planted bowls must be placed outdoors in a cool spot until growth has begun. They should then be brought indoors, but kept in complete darkness until the flower bud is showing above the neck of the bulb.
Dangers: too warm a beginning; too sudden a change; too moist a soil.
Uses: a bowl of Hyacinths is one of the most attractive of home decorations.
Propagation: from seeds, sown as soon as they ripen. Species will take two or three years to flower.

Hippeastrum

NARCISSUS SPECIES

Family Amaryllidaceae. A genus of 60 species of tunicated bulbs.
Habit: a wide range of trumpet-flowered bulbs in yellow, white, pink and orange.
Description: there are many types of narcissi and this popular bulb flower is easy to grow indoors and out, although some grow better than others indoors. Again they should have a period of vernalization and be brought indoors in darkness only when flower buds are visible. After flowering plant outdoors.
Needs: vernalization; keep soil moist but not wet.
Dangers: one should not hasten the necessary gradual process of growing narcissi indoors.
Uses: a bowl of indoor daffodils is a sign of the welcome spring to come.
Propagation: after narcissi have been growing outdoors they will produce offsets. These can be separated and graded for use.

Narcissus

TULIP

(*Tulipa* species)
Family Liliaceae. A genus of 100 species of hardy bulbs.
Habit: goblet-shaped flowers with six petals growing from a pointed bulb.
Description: there are many varieties of tulips, not all of which can successfully be grown in the home. Suitable types usually need about 10-12 weeks of vernalization before being brought indoors to a dark place with a temperature of about 15°C (60°F) to get good stem length. Tulips seem to prefer soil to bulb fibre or water and pebbles.
Needs: plenty of water when in full flower, then less until the bulbs are transferred to the garden after flowering.
Dangers: too brief a period of vernalization; too hasty a move into light and warmth; too wet or dry a soil.
Use: tulips are always bright and can be used alone or to give colour to a mixed arrangement.
Propagation: take offsets from bulbs in the garden, dry them and plant later to develop gradually to flowering size.

Tulips may not be the to grow indoors but they are among the brightest.

GLOSSARY

Aerial roots roots that grow from stems above soil level.
Annual plant grown from seed that flowers and fruits the same year.
Areole a tiny lump arising in a leaf axil in cacti, bearing spines or hairs.
Bract modified leaf around a flower.
Bromeliad member of Bromeliaceae family, usually with spiny leaves, e.g. pineapple.
Bulb storage organ with complete plant packed into its centre.
Bulbil small bulb, sometimes produced above ground level.
Cache pot decorative waterproof pot to contain the plant pot with a moist and water absorbent layer between the two.
Corm underground storage organ.
Corolla the coloured petals of a flower.
Crenated with shallow, rounded teeth.
Decumbent horizontal or prostrate stems with upright tips.
Epiphyte plant growing above ground, usually on a tree branch, but not a parasite.
Family the subsequent unit of classification above genus, ending in *ae* or *eae*.
Glaucous blue-grey or blue-green.
Glochid barbed bristle growing from the areoles of some cacti.
Habit the general style of growth of a plant: tall, short, prostrate.
Herb plant with non-woody stems.
Humus organic matter resulting from the decay of plant and animal matter.
Hybrid plant developed by crossing two species, or rarely, genera.
Inflorescence the grouping of flowers on a plant.
Involucre the surround of bracts to a cluster of flowers or florets.
Lanceolate shaped like a spear.
Lateral side shoot.
Node where leaf joins stem.
Offset young plant or modified shoot growing at the foot of a mature plant.
Perennial any plant that lives for several or many years.
Perlite inert, sterile mineral in the form of tiny white balls used to lighten and improve soil mixtures.
Pinna, Pinnae the leaflet(s) of a pinnate leaf.
Pinnate leaf divided into two lines of smaller leaves on each side of the midrib.
Raceme inflorescence comprising a steam bearing stalked flowers.
Rhizome underground horizontal stem.
Rosette circle of leaves growing outwards from ground level or at the top of a stem as with a palm tree.
Runner thin prostrate stem which will root at nodes and tip.
Scape long, leafless, flowering stem such as a daffodil.
Sessile stalk- or stem-less.
Spandix fleshy flower spike made up of many tiny flowers.
Spathe coloured bract enclosing one or more flowers.
Species group of plants which interbreed and have basically similar characteristics.
Sphagnum moss bog moss, almost sterile and highly water-retentive.
Stellata star-like, with radiating petals, bracts or branches.
Stolon aerial stem which will root when it touches the soil.
Succulent plant with either swollen leaves or stems containing water retentive tissue.
Terrestrial growing on the ground as opposed to epiphytic, on trees.
Transpire to lose water by evaporation through the stomata or leaf pores.
Tuber underground storage organ in the form of a swollen stem or root.
Umbel inflorescence of stalked flowers all rising from the same point.
Variegated plant with white or yellow spots, streaks or blotches on leaves due to lack of chlorophyll in one or more layers of leaf tissue.
Variety division in the classification of plants, a sub-division of a species.
Vernalization the practice of cooling or giving an artificial winter to a plant, bulb or seed in order to obtain early growth or flowering.

INDEX

(English Names)

African Hemp 70
African Violet 22, 102
Aloe, Partridge-
  Breasted 107
Aluminium Plant 62
Amaryllis 120
Angel's Tears 90
Angel's Wings 30
Aspidistra *see* Cast
  Iron Plant
Azalea 14, 88

Begonia 23, 29, 88
Blood Leaf 54
Blue-Flowered
  Torch 104
Bird's Nest 56
Blushing Bromeliad 56
Busy Lizzie 11, 99

Calamondin Orange 94
Cape Heath 96
Cape Primrose 104
Cast Iron Plant 28
Castor Oil Plant 42
Century Plant 106
Cherry, Winter 102, 103
Chinese Evergreen 26
Christmas Cactus 116
Chrysanthemum
  Hybrids 92, 93
Clog Plant 99
Coleus 35
Column Cactus 109
Crab Cactus 117
Crocus,
  Autumn 118, 119
  Species 119
Croton 34, 35
Crown of Thorns 112
Cyclamen 14, 95

Dumb Cane 38

Earth Star 36
Easter Cactus 116
Elephant's Ear 60
Emerald Ripple 58

False Aralia 38
Ferns 76
Fig Family 44
Flaming Dragontree 36
Flaming Katy 113
Flaming Sword 105
Flamingo Flower 86
Fuchsia 96

Geranium 22, 100
Gloxinia 97
Golden Barrel Cactus 112
Goldfinger Cactus 114
Goldfish Plant 94
Goose Foot Plant 72
Greek Vase Plant 86

Hearts Entwined 109
Hot Water Plant 85
Hyacinth 120
Hydrangea 98

Iron Cross Begonia 29
Italian Bellflower 91
Ivy 11, 18, 23, 51
  Cape 69
  Devil's 68
  German 69
  Grape 64
  Swedish 63

Japanese Sedge 32
Japanese Spindle
  Tree 40
Jasmine 100

Lily, Boat 64
     Kaffir 118

Madagascar Dragon
  Tree 40
Maple, Flowering 85
Mind Your Own
  Business 52
Moon Valley Plant 62
Mother-in-Law's
  Tongue 11, 65
Mother of Thousands 108

Narcissus 121

Norfolk Island Pine 28

Old Man Cactus 108
Opuntia Species 115

Palms 82
Parasol Plant 52
Peacock Plant 31
Pick-a-Back Plant 73
Pin Cushion Cactus 114
Pineapple, Variegated 26
Poinsettia 14, 41
Polka Dot Plant 53
Prayer Plant 54
Primula 101
Privet, Desert 59

Rat's Tail Cactus 107
Rebutia Species 115
Ribbon Plant 39
Rubber Plant 9, 23, 45

Saucer Plant 106
Silver Torch Cactus 110
Shrimp Plant 89
Silvery Inch Plant 74
Slipper Flower 91
Snakeskin Plant 48
Spider Plant 33
Spleenwort 77
Strawberry Geranium 66
Sweetheart Plant 61
Swiss Cheese Plant 55

Tree Philodendron 60
Tulip 121

Umbrella Grass 37
Umbrella Plant 67

Vine, Chestnut 12
      Kangaroo 34
      Purple Passion 49

Wandering Jew 75
Wax Flower 97
White Sails 103
Winter Cherry 102

Yucca, Spineless 74

Zebra Plant 87

(Scientific Names)

Abutilon striatum thompsonii 85
Achimenes hybrids 85
Adiantum capillus-veneris 76
Aechmea fasciata 76
Aeonium tabuliforme 106
Agave americana 106
Aglaonema commutatum 26
Aloe variegata 107
Ananas bracteatus striatus 26
Aporocactus flagelliformis 107
Anthurium scherzerianum 86
Aphelandra squarrosa louisae 87
Araucaria excelsa 28
Asparagus plumosus 76
Aspidistra elatior 28
Asplenium bulbiferum 77
  nidus 77
Azalea indica 88

Begonia masoniana 29
  rex 30
  species 88
Billbergia nutans 90
Bougainvillea glabra 90
Bryophyllum daigremontianum 108

Caladium bicolor 30
Calathea species 31
Calceolaria herbeohybrida 91
Campanula alba 91
Carex morrowii variegata 32
Cephalocereus senilis 108
Cereus peruvianus 109
Ceropegia woodii 109
Chlorophytum comosum 33
Cineraria cruenta 93

Cissus antarctica 24
Citrus mitis 94
Cleistocactus straussii 110
Clivia miniata 118
Cocos weddeliana 82
Codiaeum variegatum pictum 34, 35
Colchicum byzantinum 118, 119
Columnea banksii 94
Cordyline australis 36
  terminalis 36
Crassula species 110
Cryptanthus bromelioides tricolor 36
Cycas revoluta 83
Cyclamen persicum 95
Cyperus alternifolius 37
Cyrtomium falcatum 78

Dieffenbachia picta 38
Dizygotheca elegantissima 38
Dracaena concinna 40
  marginata 40
  sanderiana 39
  tricolor 40
Dryopteris filix-mas 78

Echeveria species 111
Echinocactus grusonii 112
Erica hyemalis 96
Euonymus japonicus 40, 41
Euphorbia milii 112
  pulcherrima 41
  splendens 112

Fatshedera lizei 42
Fatsia japonica 42
Ficus
  benjamina 44
  diversifolia 44
  elastica decora 45
  lyrata 45
  pumila 46
  radicans variegata 47

Fittonia argyroneura 48
  verschaffeltii 48
Fuchsia hybrids 96

Gynura aurantiaca 49
  sarmentosa 49

Hedera species 50
Helxine soleirolii 52, 53
Heptapleurum arboricola 52
Howea forsteriana 83
Hoya carnosa 97
Hydrangea varieties 98
Hypocyrta glabra 99
Hypoëstes sanguinolenta 53

Impatiens holstii 11
Iresine herbstii 54

Jasminum polyanthum 100

Kalanchoe blossfeldiana 113
Kentia forsteriana 83

Mammillaria bocasana 114
Maranta leuconeura 54, 55

Neanthe bella 84
Neoregelia carolinae tricolor 56
Nephrolepis exaltata bostoniensis 78, 79
Nidularium innocentii 56
Notocactus leninghausii 114

Opuntia species 115

Pandanus veitchii 57
Pelargonium varieties 100
Pellionia pulchra 58
Peperomia argyreia 58
  caperata 59
  magnoliae folia 59
  sandersii 58

Philodendron
  bipinnatifidum 60
  scandens 61
  tuxla 61
Phoenix dactylifera 84
Phyllitis
  scolopendrium 79
Pilea cadierei 62
  mollis
Platycerium
  bifurcatum 80
Plectranthus
  oertendahlii 63
Primula species 101
Pteris albolineata 81
  cretica 81
  Wimsettii 81

Rebutia miniscula 115
Rhipsalidopsis rosea 116
Rhoeo discolor 64
Rhoicissus
  rhomboidea 64

Saintpaulia
  ionantha 102
Sansevieria hahnii 65
  trifasciata laurentii
    11, 65, 66
Saxifraga sarmentosa 66
Schefflera
  actinophylla 67
Schlumbergera
  gaertneri 116
Scindapsus aureus 68
Sedum
  pachyphyllum 117
  sieboldii 116, 117
Selaginella aurea 81
  kraussiana 81
Senecio macroglossus
  variegatus 69
  mikanoides 69
Sinningia speciosa 97
Solanum
  capsicastrum 102
Sparmannia africana 70

Spathiphyllum
  wallisii 103
Streptocarpus
  hybrids 104
Stromanthe amabilis 70
Syngonium
  podophyllum 72

Tetrastigma
  vionierianum 72
Tillandsia cyanea 104
Tolmeia menziesii 73
Tradescantia species 74
Vriesia splendens 105
Yucca elephantipes 74

Zebrina pendula 75
  quadricolor 75
Zygocactus
  truncatus 117

The Publishers wish to thank the following for their kind help in supplying photographs for this book:

Heather Angel: pages 35, 77, 78, 80. **Ministry of Agriculture, Fisheries & Food. Crown copyright**: pages 18, 19. **A-Z Collection**: pages 43, 59, 81, 89, 103, 106, 108, 109, 114, 117, 119 left. **Bruce Coleman**: page 25. **Eric Crichton/Natural Science Photos**: pages 95, 97, 99, 104, 105. **Mary Evans Picture Library**: pages 8, 9. **Hamlyn Group**: page 98. **Leslie Johns**: pages 39, 53, 68, Bottom, 96. **The Original New Leaf Partnership/Rod Shone, from Complete Indoor Gardener by Pan**: 49, 65, 66, 79. **House of Rochford**: pages 91, 94. **Harry Smith**: pages 47, 51, 54, 85, 87, 92, 93, 101, 107, 110, 112, 116, 119 right, 120, 121. **Vision International**: page 36.
All other photographs taken specially by Paul Forrester.
Picture Research: Penny Warn.